How to Draw
Cute Doodles
and Illustrations

A Step-by-Step Beginner's Guide

KAMO

TUTTLE Publishing

Tokyo | Rutland, Vermont | Singapore

CONTENTS

PART 1 Let's Draw Basic Illustrations

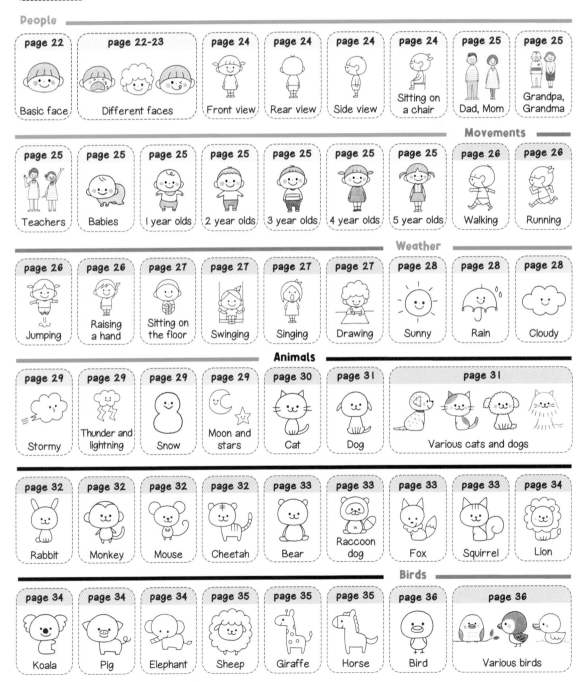

People

page 22	page 22-23	page 24	page 24	page 24	page 24	page 25	page 25
Basic face	Different faces	Front view	Rear view	Side view	Sitting on a chair	Dad, Mom	Grandpa, Grandma

Movements

page 25	page 25	page 25	page 25	page 25	page 25	page 25	page 26	page 26
Teachers	Babies	1 year olds	2 year olds	3 year olds	4 year olds	5 year olds	Walking	Running

Weather

page 26	page 26	page 27	page 27	page 27	page 27	page 28	page 28	page 28
Jumping	Raising a hand	Sitting on the floor	Swinging	Singing	Drawing	Sunny	Rain	Cloudy

Animals

page 29	page 29	page 29	page 29	page 30	page 31	page 31
Stormy	Thunder and lightning	Snow	Moon and stars	Cat	Dog	Various cats and dogs

page 32	page 32	page 32	page 32	page 33	page 33	page 33	page 33	page 34
Rabbit	Monkey	Mouse	Cheetah	Bear	Raccoon dog	Fox	Squirrel	Lion

Birds

page 34	page 34	page 34	page 35	page 35	page 35	page 36	page 36
Koala	Pig	Elephant	Sheep	Giraffe	Horse	Bird	Various birds

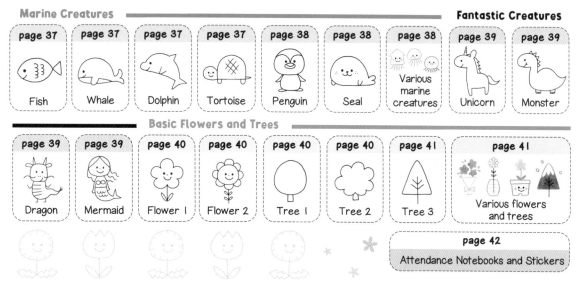
PART 2 Let's Draw Illustrations for the Twelve Months of the Year

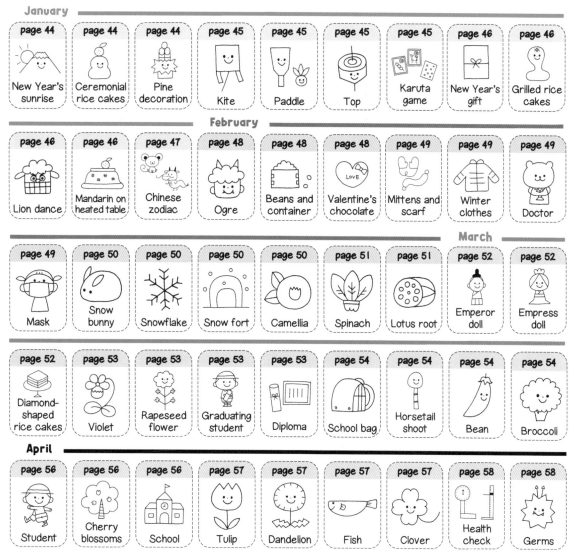

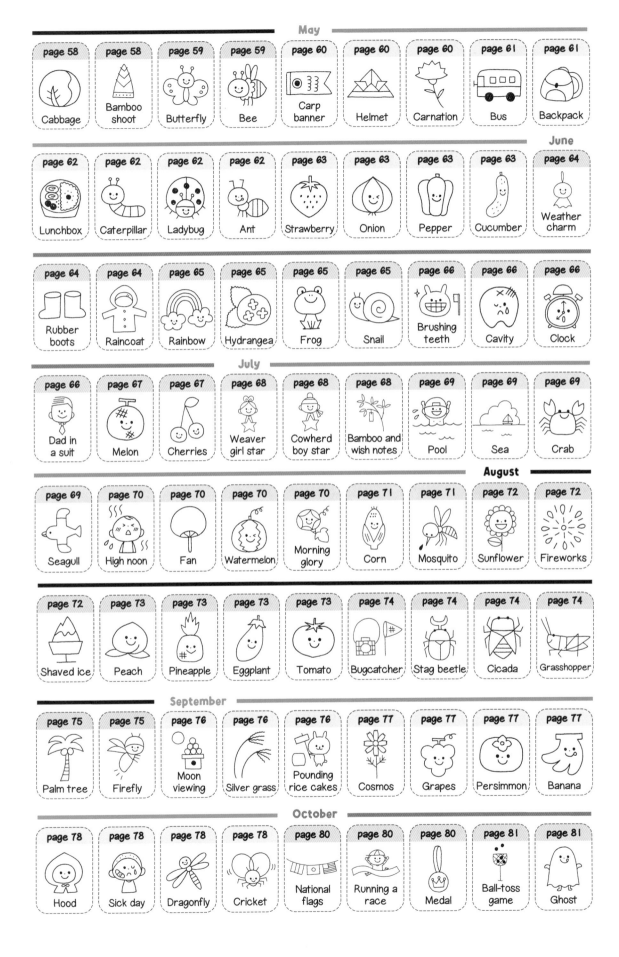

May

page 58	page 58	page 59	page 59	page 60	page 60	page 60	page 61	page 61
Cabbage	Bamboo shoot	Butterfly	Bee	Carp banner	Helmet	Carnation	Bus	Backpack

June

page 62	page 62	page 62	page 62	page 63	page 63	page 63	page 63	page 64
Lunchbox	Caterpillar	Ladybug	Ant	Strawberry	Onion	Pepper	Cucumber	Weather charm

page 64	page 64	page 65	page 65	page 65	page 65	page 66	page 66	page 66
Rubber boots	Raincoat	Rainbow	Hydrangea	Frog	Snail	Brushing teeth	Cavity	Clock

July

page 66	page 67	page 67	page 68	page 68	page 68	page 69	page 69	page 69
Dad in a suit	Melon	Cherries	Weaver girl star	Cowherd boy star	Bamboo and wish notes	Pool	Sea	Crab

August

page 69	page 70	page 70	page 70	page 70	page 71	page 71	page 72	page 72
Seagull	High noon	Fan	Watermelon	Morning glory	Corn	Mosquito	Sunflower	Fireworks

page 72	page 73	page 73	page 73	page 73	page 74	page 74	page 74	page 74
Shaved ice	Peach	Pineapple	Eggplant	Tomato	Bugcatcher	Stag beetle	Cicada	Grasshopper

September

page 75	page 75	page 76	page 76	page 76	page 77	page 77	page 77	page 77
Palm tree	Firefly	Moon viewing	Silver grass	Pounding rice cakes	Cosmos	Grapes	Persimmon	Banana

October

page 78	page 78	page 78	page 78	page 80	page 80	page 80	page 81	page 81
Hood	Sick day	Dragonfly	Cricket	National flags	Running a race	Medal	Ball-toss game	Ghost

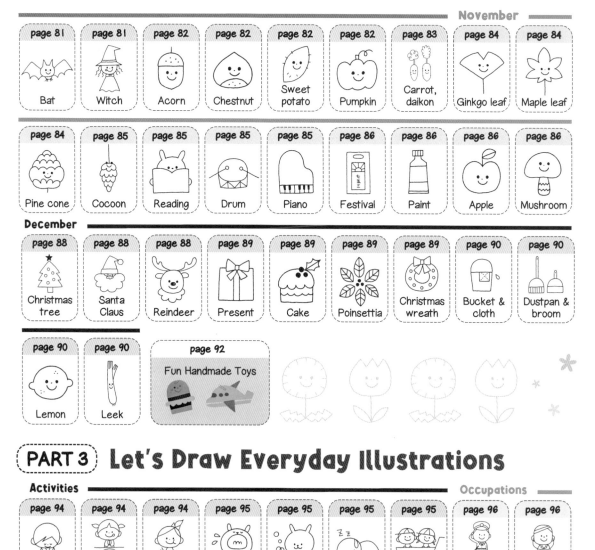

page 81	page 81	page 82	page 82	page 82	page 82	page 83	page 84	page 84
Bat	Witch	Acorn	Chestnut	Sweet potato	Pumpkin	Carrot, daikon	Ginkgo leaf	Maple leaf
page 84	page 85	page 85	page 85	page 85	page 86	page 86	page 86	page 86
Pine cone	Cocoon	Reading	Drum	Piano	Festival	Paint	Apple	Mushroom

December

page 88	page 88	page 88	page 89	page 89	page 89	page 89	page 90	page 90
Christmas tree	Santa Claus	Reindeer	Present	Cake	Poinsettia	Christmas wreath	Bucket & cloth	Dustpan & broom
page 90	page 90	page 92						
Lemon	Leek	Fun Handmade Toys						

PART 3 Let's Draw Everyday Illustrations

Activities   Occupations

page 94	page 94	page 94	page 95	page 95	page 95	page 95	page 96	page 96
Greetings	Bon appetit!	Eating	Gargling	Washing	Nap	Stroller	Police officer	Doctor
page 96	page 97	page 97	page 97	page 97	page 98	page 98	page 98	page 98
Nurse	Firefighter	Conductor	Performer	Chef	Waitress	Astronaut	Soccer player	Baseball player

Stories

page 99	page 99	page 99	page 99	page 100	page 100	page 100	page 101	page 101
Baker	Scientist	Florist	Fishmonger	Castle	Princess	Prince	Pirate	Ninja

Food

page 101	page 101	page 102	page 102	page 102	page 103	page 103	page 103	page 103
Red Riding Hood	Wolf	Birthday cake	Shortcake	Cupcake	Milk	Pudding	Pancakes	Soft serve

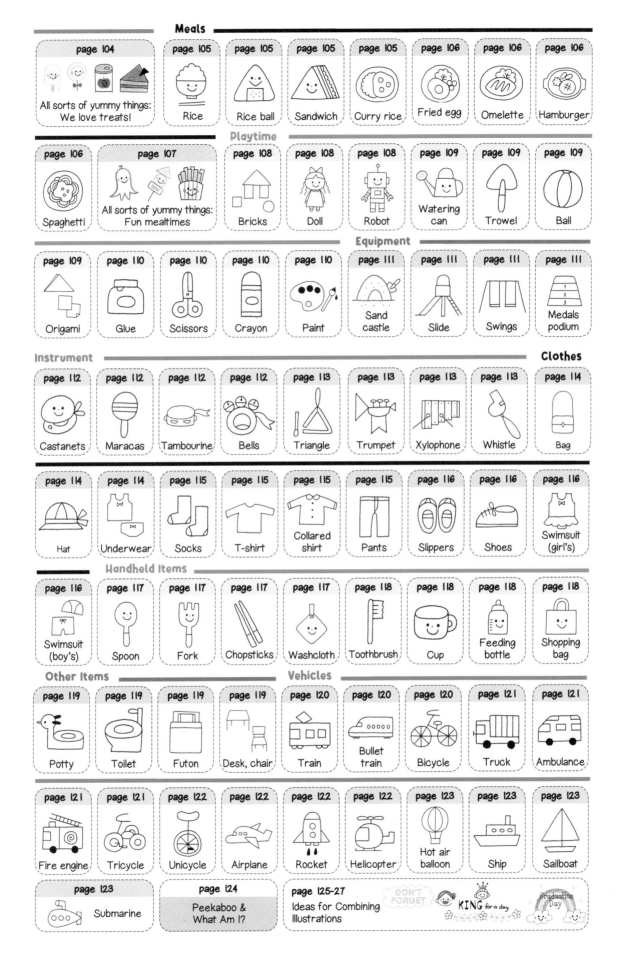

DON'T FORGET
KING for a day
Graduation Day

So cute! Kids will love them!
How to Use Your Illustrations

Teaming the drawings with flowers adds dimension. When drawing on the blackboard, step away occasionally to check the overall balance.

Blackboard

How to get good results on a blackboard

Before starting to draw, roughly picture the position and size of your drawing for a well-balanced result.

For drawings and text that you want to stand out against the blackboard, use white, yellow and pink chalk.

Use the end of the chalk for a fine line or lay it on its side for a thick line.

Blackboard   school = p.56, cherry blossoms = p.56, full body (front view) = p.24, hat for wearing to school = p.114

How to make small tissue paper flowers

Layer five pieces of tissue paper and cut in half, then fold into pleats at about ⁵/₈" (1.5cm) intervals.

KEY POINT

Use mountain folds at the start and end of the pleating.

Staple at the center and use scissors to round the ends.

Fluff out the petals. Round out the petals at the bottom for a cute look.

✱The bicolored flowers are made by layering three sheets of orange tissue paper and two of yellow and using scissors to round the ends of the paper.

Posters

Use large letters for the part that you want to emphasize. Using familiar icons makes it easy to understand.

Expert Tip

As this is to be hung near water, laminating it keeps it dry and protected!

Poster   rabbit washing hands = p.95, germs = p.58, faucet = p.95

Use white-ink pens on dark colored paper. For slightly tricky illustrations, draw them on a different sheet of paper, then stick them to the poster to avoid mistakes.

Poster

4th of **July**

FIREWORKS DISPLAY
8 to 10 P.M.

Bring a blanket or a lawn chair! ✦✦

Using colored pencils creates a gentle, soft look. You can affix colored paper to important parts of the poster.

Poster

July 1st

BABY Shower
10:00 ₺ 12:00
Midtown Café

Is it a BOY or a GIRL?

Gender reveal and refreshments

ELEMENTARY SCHOOL LOTTERY

Ticket

Adding in characters creates a sense of fun.

JULY 22nd
Support the Band
First Prize $100

JULY 22nd
Support the Band
First Prize $100

JULY 22nd
Support the Band
First Prize $100

Poster: 4th of July   fireworks = p.72, fan = p.70
Poster: baby shower   bricks = p.108, robot = p.108, ball = p.109, T-shirt = p.115, spoon, fork = p.117, shopping bag = p.118, cupcake = p.102, candy = p.104, boots = p.64
Ticket   rabbit = p.32

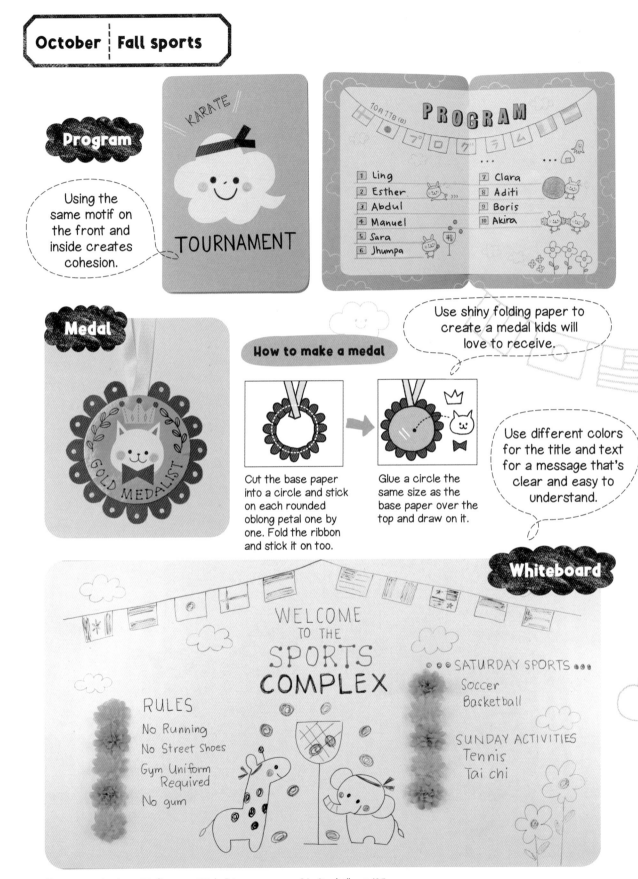

Program

Using the same motif on the front and inside creates cohesion.

KARATE
TOURNAMENT

PROGRAM

1. Ling
2. Esther
3. Abdul
4. Manuel
5. Sara
6. Jhumpa
7. Clara
8. Aditi
9. Boris
10. Akira

Medal

GOLD MEDALIST

Use shiny folding paper to create a medal kids will love to receive.

How to make a medal

Cut the base paper into a circle and stick on each rounded oblong petal one by one. Fold the ribbon and stick it on too.

Glue a circle the same size as the base paper over the top and draw on it.

Use different colors for the title and text for a message that's clear and easy to understand.

Whiteboard

WELCOME TO THE SPORTS COMPLEX

RULES
No Running
No Street Shoes
Gym Uniform Required
No gum

SATURDAY SPORTS
Soccer
Basketball

SUNDAY ACTIVITIES
Tennis
Tai chi

Program   cloud = p.28, flags = p.80, ball-toss game = p.81, rice ball = p.105
Medal   cat = p.30
Whiteboard   flags = p.80, cloud = p.28, ball-toss game = p.81, giraffe = p.35, elephant = p.34

Posters

Paste base paper onto the back for a neat finish. Simply adding round dot stickers adds to the overall look.

Pop-up card

Come to the
★ MAGIC SHOW ★

Saturday
December **11**th
3 - 5 p.m.

ART

🎖 Gallery Opening 10 - 2 p.m.

🎖 Auction & Reception afterward

Thick cardstock has been used under the animal figure for a raised look.

How to make a pop-up card

Mountain fold   cut
Valley fold

Cut and fold paper as per the diagram above. Use pinking shears around the edges if you like.

Assemble as per the diagram above. Glue a slightly larger piece of paper to the back for a neat finish.

Affix the paper with the drawing on it to the front. This is the pop-up part of the card.

Attach the parts with drawings and text along with the dot stickers to complete!

Poster   ginkgo leaf = p.84, maple leaf = p.84, paints = p.110
Pop-up card   ribbon frame = p.15, rabbit = p.32

Birthday party

This is a fun card with pages to turn, like in a picture book.

Front

HAPPY **6**th

HEALTH FAIR
115 cm
18 kg
Vision and Hearing Test

Back

May all your Dreams come true!

Card

Use ribbon for a three-dimensional look! Adding a picture of the child makes it a gift she'll love.

Front

HAPPY **6** BIRTHDAY

Back

HAPPY BIRTHDAY

How to make a medal

Curve the ribbon as per the diagram and use tape to hold it in place. Make six of these.

Glue the six pieces of ribbon and a piece of ribbon with the ends trimmed into inverted Vs to the round base. Stick the circle of paper with text and illustration over the top.

Medal

Card giraffe = p.35, health check = p.58, elephant = p.34, heart = p.15, spaghetti = p.106, mandarin = p.46, ogre = p.48, crayon = p.110, rabbit = p.32
Medal 6 = p.126

Newsletters

4th Grade SCHOOL NEWS Tel : 123-456

Mint eost, consecum autemquia pera eostiati odist, cum faccupt atemped magnis as debit mi, sam re velic toreria temolor ruptatem se et, cumque excea vero coreptia pore mo qui nessendusam arunditet a nihilles expedi ut alia ventiate demperio cum conesse quiatem

4 Your text here

8	Your text here
13 ~ 15	Your text here
21	Your text here
23	Your text here

Your text here .... Ur ratempo stiosapisit, quis rem. Faccuscia

4 Your text here

★ Your text here → Ad molorum essum fugit qui abo. Aditemos
★ Your text here → Ad molorum essum fugit qui abo. Aditemos
★ Your text here → Ad molorum essum fugit qui abo. Aditemos

Udit, untiate est aces eos descipit fugit, cusae veligniscit ipsa cus, vendi blandam que nimenda sum, conet volorem facea prate prem is am, sustisc ipienti del escillum

Your text here

T E X T
··· Your text here ···
☐ Your text here
☐ Your text here
☐ Your text here

T E X T

Your text here — Sum dolor auditat. Itin ped quianduciunt hitaspero eic te
Your text here — Sum dolor auditat. Itin ped quianduciunt hitaspero eic te
Your text here — Sum dolor auditat. Itin ped quianduciunt hitaspero eic te

Letters in white catch the eye, but don't overuse them.

Use different sizes and styles of boxes to make the page easy to understand at a glance.

PULSE OF THE PEOPLE APRIL

Pos ex et volendi dolorrum eati ipiciet estrumendita sit quuntore nus volo excerit es es explisquatae prae et et receprorem aceatent verum remquam que endae litat

Text here
Ipsam quassitate lanimusci des accae prorunt aut et ipsus des accae prorunt aut et

T E X T
Ipsam quassitate lanimusci des
Acite prat liant. Hictat reptati qui rehenet ommolup tatempo reptam quid et ut ra exernam nonsequam, autenis incipsae. Ci apiscium ea si aut unt.

Ipsam quassitate
Acite prat liant. Hictat reptati qui rehenet ommolup tatempo reptam quid et ut ra exernam nonsequam, autenis incipsae. Ci apiscium ea si aut unt.

Aximusae sam rerum la con resslicte paria culeati nonet

Your Text here
Ipsam quassitate lanimusci des accae prorunt aut et ipsus des accae prorunt aut et

Your Text here
Tum as maximet as voluptae. Itae. Nam quias ducil iducit is ma voluptae mosanis dit volestio officim earchit mi, simodit iorestrum que comnia volum que aut a voiescimet lacerrumquam litatiae voluptaquam aut anf ame eria diciam incilicto quatur?

School newsletter tulip = p.57, cherry blossoms = p.56, butterfly = p.59, school = p.56, health check = p.58, birthday cake = p.102, hood = p.78, T-shirt = p.115, socks = p.115, shoes = p.116, horsetail shoot = p.54, cat = p.30, basic face = p.22, different faces = p.22-23
Health insurance newsletter nurse = p.96, dandelion and fluff = p.57, health check = p.58, T-shirt = p.115, pants = p.115, clock = p.66

Let's Try Drawing Lines

Simply adding decorative lines to drawings and text or using lines around them creates a sense of fun.

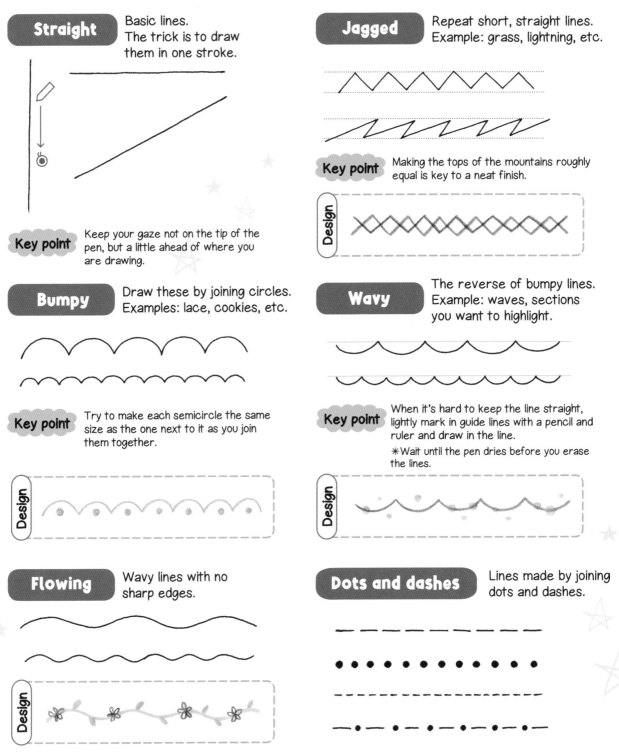

Straight

Basic lines.
The trick is to draw them in one stroke.

Key point Keep your gaze not on the tip of the pen, but a little ahead of where you are drawing.

Bumpy

Draw these by joining circles. Examples: lace, cookies, etc.

Key point Try to make each semicircle the same size as the one next to it as you join them together.

Design

Flowing

Wavy lines with no sharp edges.

Design

Jagged

Repeat short, straight lines. Example: grass, lightning, etc.

Key point Making the tops of the mountains roughly equal is key to a neat finish.

Design

Wavy

The reverse of bumpy lines. Example: waves, sections you want to highlight.

Key point When it's hard to keep the line straight, lightly mark in guide lines with a pencil and ruler and draw in the line.

＊Wait until the pen dries before you erase the lines.

Design

Dots and dashes

Lines made by joining dots and dashes.

Let's Try Drawing Shapes

Circles, triangles and squares are the essential building blocks. Practice until you can draw them neatly.

Circle

Start wherever you like, then it's easiest for right handers to draw in a clockwise direction, and for left handers to draw counter-clockwise.

Next level

Visualize a circle.

Use bumpy lines.

Triangle

Draw the straight lines in one stroke. If you need to rest the pen, do it at the corners.

Next level

Visualize a circle.

Use jagged lines.

Square

Make sure the corners are 90°. Draw straight lines in one stroke.

Add a pole to make a signpost.

Add thumbtacks in the corner to make an exhibition item.

Star

Draw a straight horizontal line to easily achieve a balanced look.

If you make a mistake, color in the shape to cover it up.

Next level

When you've had some practice, draw the star using only the outer lines.

Heart

Make the ★ sections rounded, with a defined center.

Rounding the base makes for a cute heart.

A pointy base creates a refined look.

Bow

Combine a square and triangles to make a bow.

Variation on a bow.

Next level

A frame made from a ribbon.

Drawing Basics

3

Choose Drawing Implements

If you have a ballpoint pen and colored pencils, you can start drawing right away.

⟦ Basic drawing tools ⟧

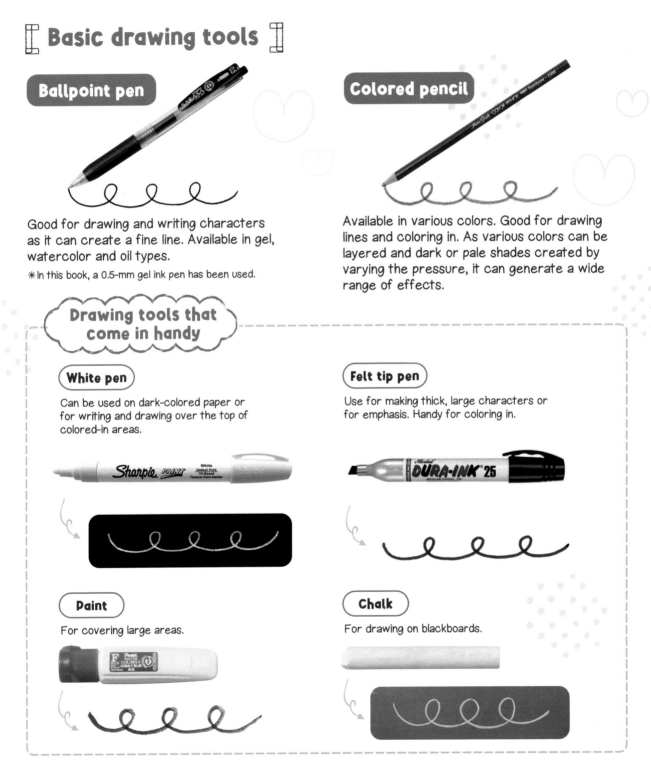

Ballpoint pen

Good for drawing and writing characters as it can create a fine line. Available in gel, watercolor and oil types.

＊In this book, a 0.5-mm gel ink pen has been used.

Colored pencil

Available in various colors. Good for drawing lines and coloring in. As various colors can be layered and dark or pale shades created by varying the pressure, it can generate a wide range of effects.

Drawing tools that come in handy

White pen

Can be used on dark-colored paper or for writing and drawing over the top of colored-in areas.

Felt tip pen

Use for making thick, large characters or for emphasis. Handy for coloring in.

Paint

For covering large areas.

Chalk

For drawing on blackboards.

Let's Add Color

Use your favorite colors to fill in or draw a pattern. Try creating your own variations.

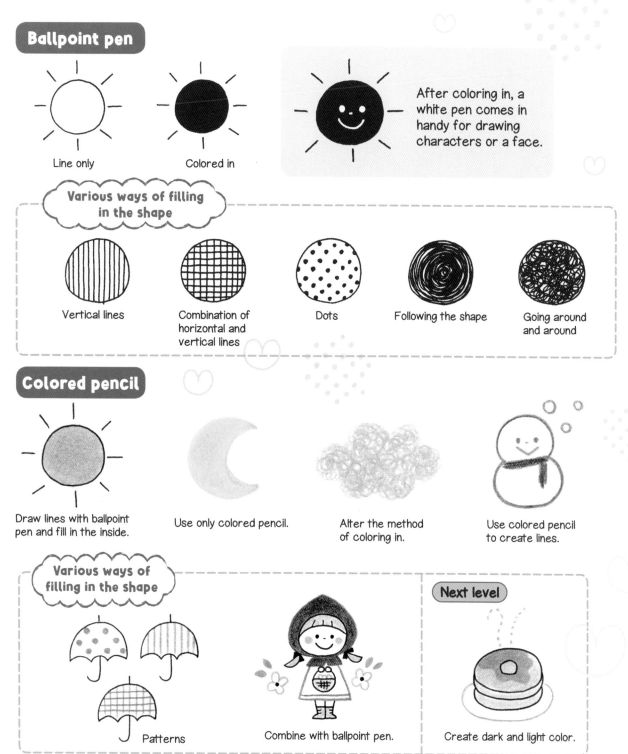

Ballpoint pen

Line only

Colored in

After coloring in, a white pen comes in handy for drawing characters or a face.

Various ways of filling in the shape

Vertical lines

Combination of horizontal and vertical lines

Dots

Following the shape

Going around and around

Colored pencil

Draw lines with ballpoint pen and fill in the inside.

Use only colored pencil.

Alter the method of coloring in.

Use colored pencil to create lines.

Various ways of filling in the shape

Patterns

Combine with ballpoint pen.

Next level

Create dark and light color.

Drawing Basics 5

Let's Try Writing Characters

It's handy to be able to create various characters in order to make posters, newsletters or signs.

Use lines and dots

Simply add lines or dots to the start and end points of characters!

Serif characters

ABCDE
12345

Characters with dots

ABCDE
67890

Use thicker vertical lines

Add emphasis to the characters by thickening the vertical sections.

Characters with thickened verticals

ABCDE
12345

Thicken and fill in the vertical sections

ABCDE
67890

Next level

Characters with thickened verticals and serifs added.

DID I DO THAT?

Thickened characters

Work the pen around and around to thicken each stroke.

/ → ┠ → A

ABCDE 1 2 3 4 5

Characters with rounded tips.

ABCDE 6 7 8 9 0

Characters with tips that are jagged as if cut.

ABCDE

Changing the color of each stroke works too.

Outlined characters

Create an outline around the characters.

Characters with squared ends

ABCDE
12345

Characters with rounded ends

ABCDE
67890

Next level Add a pattern inside

ABCDE
12345

Next level Add a shadow to create dimension.

ABCDE
67890

Add a background

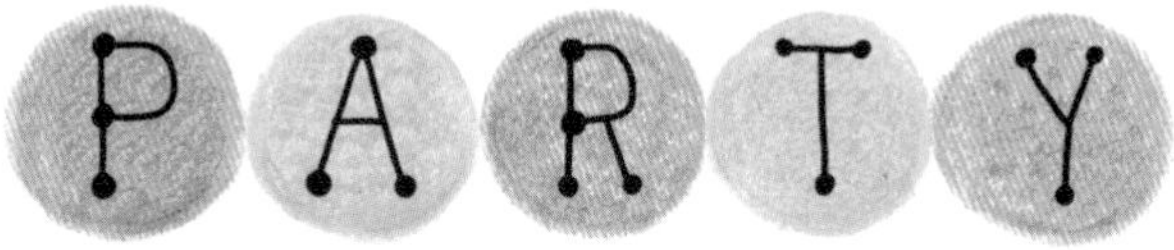

PARTY

RSVP

Speech bubbles

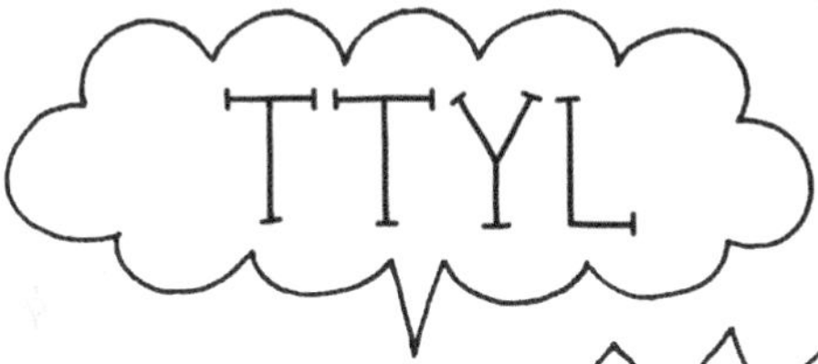

TTYL

LOL

Change the shape of the speech bubble to match the contents.

Cute symbols with faces

? ! →

How to Create Better Drawings

Visualize everyone smiling in response to your work and put your whole heart into drawing for a great result.

Tip 2

Try drawing lines all in one go

At first, drawing straight lines can be difficult. But if you pause your breath and draw the line all in one go, it works surprisingly well. It's all a matter of practice.

Tip 3

If you keep drawing, you're guaranteed to improve

Don't overthink things, just draw. There are various illustrations in this book, allowing anyone to easily draw cute pictures. Whenever you have a moment during the day, even drawing just one picture will improve your skill

Tip 1

Practice the basics

Straight lines and circles are the basics of illustration. In this book, we introduce the essentials (pp. 14-19). Daily practice will ensure your drawings improve.

Tip 4

Your enjoyment while drawing comes across to the viewer

In the same way as playing music, drawing is something to be enjoyed. If you visualize or imagine the joy and enthusiasm your drawings will create, your feelings will come through in your illustrations.

PART ONE

Let's Draw Basic Illustrations

Here, we show how to draw simple illustrations that can easily be incorporated into newsletters, posters or anything you choose. Few lines are needed to create simple illustrations of faces, cute animals, flowers, trees and more. Let's start by drawing these everyday objects.

People

For the face, start by drawing a circle. The shape of the eyes, eyebrows and mouth allows for a range of expressions to be created.

【 Faces 】 For the initial circle that forms the facial outline, it's cute to use a dumpling shape.

Basic face

Finished!

Draw a circle.　　　Add ears to both sides.　　　Add eyes, nose and mouth.

Different faces

Simply changing the hairstyle or facial outline creates a completely different look!

Part the bangs.

Add short hairs to the top of the head for a short hairstyle.

Add dots for a shaved head.

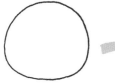

Part long bangs diagonally.

Change the hairstyle

Add triangles and a brim for a kid wearing a cap.

Change the facial outline

Rounded cheeks make for a child-like look.

Draw a triangle with a rounded chin.

Draw a square and make the chin flat.

Draw a circle and make the chin pointy.

Simple expressions

The eyes and mouth alone can create a multitude of expressions.

Enjoyment

Use < shapes for the eyes and raise the corners of the open mouth.

Crying

Use < shapes for the eyes and lower the corners of the mouth for a sad face.

Happy / asleep

Use U shapes for the eyes to make them appear closed.

Making a mistake

Use x shapes for the eyes to convey having made a mistake; "oops!"

Sleepy

Use — shapes for the eyes and open the mouth to form a circle.

"Yum" / cheeky

Use a < shape and a • to create the look of winking. Make the tongue poke out.

Cheerful / excited

Add lines to the cheeks to show anticipation, curiosity or bashfulness.

Smiling

Draw the teeth in to show delight, success or mischief.

Complicated expressions

Adding in eyebrows allows for the creation of more complex expressions.

Confusion

Lowering one eyebrow creates a look of confusion or worry.

Anger

Raise the eyebrows to express anger. Color the cheeks red.

Unsettled

Make the eyebrows form a swirling shape and use a wavy line for the mouth.

Discomfort

Raise both eyebrows, draw a bead of sweat and make the mouth open and twisted to depict fretting or impatience.

More!

Hairstyle variations

Draw only the lower part of the facial outline, then draw in the hair.

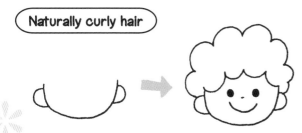

Naturally curly hair

Draw the lower half of a circle and add bushy hair.

A girl with hair covering her ears

Draw the lower half of a circle and let the hair hang down, omitting the ears.

〚 Full length 〛 A large head makes for a child-like look.

Front view   This is how to draw the standard front-on view.

\ Finished! /

From shoulders to wrists.

From underarms to skirt hem.

Both arms and the base of the neck.

Draw in the legs and feet to complete.

Rear view   Apart from not adding the face, it's the same as drawing the front view.

\ Finished! /

Don't draw the face.

If separating the upper and lower garments, draw from the underarms to the hips.

For pants, add a line in the center.

Draw in the legs and feet to complete.

Side view   Simply adding the nose on the side creates the base.

\ Finished! /

Add the nose to point in the direction you want the head to face.

Keep the curve of the chest and belly in mind.

Draw the arms extending from the shoulders.

When completely in profile, it's fine to just draw the closest leg!

Sitting on a chair   Create a letter H to make drawing the chair easy.

\ Finished! /

Create a bend in the body from the hips down.

Bend the arms to place the hands on the knees.

Draw the chair.

Draw the legs and feet to complete!

24

People we love

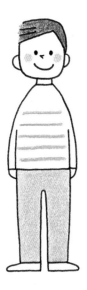

Dad

Face: square or long
    for an adult look
Shoulders: broad
Neck: thick
Legs: slightly apart

Mom

Face: longer than
    a child's
Shoulders: narrow
Neck: thin
Legs: together

Grandpa & Grandma

Hair: gray or white
Face: wrinkled
Back: rounded
Limbs: slightly bent

Teacher

Physique: adult male and
    female
Expression: cheerful
Gestures: active and
    healthy
Attire: easy to move

Babies - 5 year olds

Babies Draw minimal hair, short limbs and a rounded belly and bottom.

One year olds

Bend the limbs for a waddling effect.

Two year olds

Extend the hands for a balanced look.

Three year olds

The limbs are short, but the child is in control of his movements.

Four year olds

Use the hairstyle and clothing to distinguish between girls and boys.

Five year olds

Make the limbs longer and the figure taller.

〖 Movements 〗

Walking
Make sure to show the opposite arm and leg.

\ Finished! /

A simple walking pose.

Running
The figure leans forward more than when walking and the limbs are bent.

\ Finished! /

Make the arms and legs asymmetrical for an action pose.

Jumping
Depicting the legs as being bent and rounded is key.

\ Finished! /

Add a rope and rounded hands for a figure jumping rope.

Raising a hand
Separating the thumb from the other fingers creates the look of an open hand.

\ Finished! /

Draw two lines to depict waving.

Sitting on the floor

Bend both the elbows to show that the figure is holding his knees.

\ Finished! /

Adding color and creating variation

When the legs are extended, position them to show that the soles of the feet are fully in view.

Swinging

Bend the elbows, open out the arms and bend the knees.

\ Finished! /

Adding color and creating variation

Positioning the facial features higher up on the face creates the impression of looking upward.

Singing

Open the mouth wide, bend the elbows and bring the arms to the back.

\ Finished! /

Adding color and creating variation

Alter the shape of the eyes and mouth to vary the expression.

Drawing

Drawing the facial features lower on the face creates the impression of looking down.

\ Finished! /

Adding color and creating variation

Scattering pencils around makes for a realistic look.

Weather

Weather symbols are great seasonal appropriate additions to calendars, diaries and flyers. Add faces to create a wealth of expressions.

Sunny Tweak the lines around the circle! For days with gentle sunshine, use small lines, with bigger ones for gloriously sunny days.

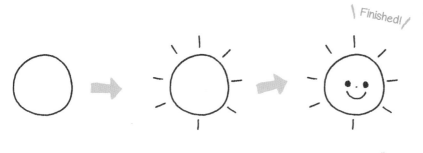

\ Finished! /

Adding color and creating variation

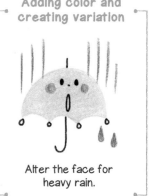

Use colored pencil for the facial outline too.

Rain Make the dome of the umbrella deep for a cute effect.

\ Finished! /

Adding color and creating variation

Alter the face for heavy rain.

Cloudy Make the rounded edges as if joining circles together.

\ Finished! /

Adding color and creating variation

Use a diagonal line for clouds followed by rain.

Stormy

Change the bottom part of the cloud and add pursed lips to suggest the wind blowing.

\ Finished! /

Thunder and lightning

Draw light coming from the cloud to show lightning, with fangs to indicate thunder.

\ Finished! /

Snow

Don't make the top and bottom balls different sizes, so your snowman is plump but balanced.

\ Finished! /

Moon and stars

Visualize a circle to draw the moon. Add a star to make a set.

\ Finished! /

\ Finished! /

29

Animals

Just like for drawing people, start with a round face when drawing creatures. Create different animals and looks by altering the ears, tail and fur.

〖 Cats & dogs 〗

Cat front

\ Finished! /

Draw a circle with triangles for the ears. Join the nose to the mouth.

Use a rounded teardrop for the body.

Position the front legs together.

Add the tail to complete the picture!
*Add whiskers if you like.

Cat profile

\ Finished! /

Add the nose in the direction you want the cat to face.

Draw the front legs.

Draw the hind legs and make a smooth back.

Add the tail to complete the picture!
*Add whiskers if you like.

Kitten and parent

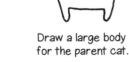

For a kitten, make the face big and the body small. You can make the ears and facial features large!

Draw a large body for the parent cat.

Joining the circle to the triangles as you draw makes for a simpler look.

Small dog

Draw a circle with drooping ears. Make the body slightly solid.

Side

Front view

Show part of the hind legs when drawing the front view. Visualize the front legs as being apart rather than close together.

Large dog

Giving a circle rounded "corners" creates the look of a large dog. Make the body large too.

Front view

For large dogs, when drawing in profile, lengthen the snout and make the body large.

Profile

Various cats and dogs

● Cat sitting upright

● Long-haired cat

● Running cat

● Napping cat

● Spotted dog
* It's good to add a collar too.

● Fluffy dog

● Funny dog

● Dog with ears pricked

〘 Animals 〙

Rabbit   The key is to draw the ears long.

\ Finished! /

Bending the ears makes for a cute look.

Monkey   Add round ears to the sides and draw an "m" shape on the forehead.

\ Finished! /

Add movement to the limbs if you like!

Mouse   Make the ears large, the mouth slightly narrow and add a long tail.

\ Finished! /

With cheese, a mouse's favorite treat.

Cheetah   The cheetah is defined by the spots on its head and body.

\ Finished! /

Change the pattern to spots to turn it into a cheetah!

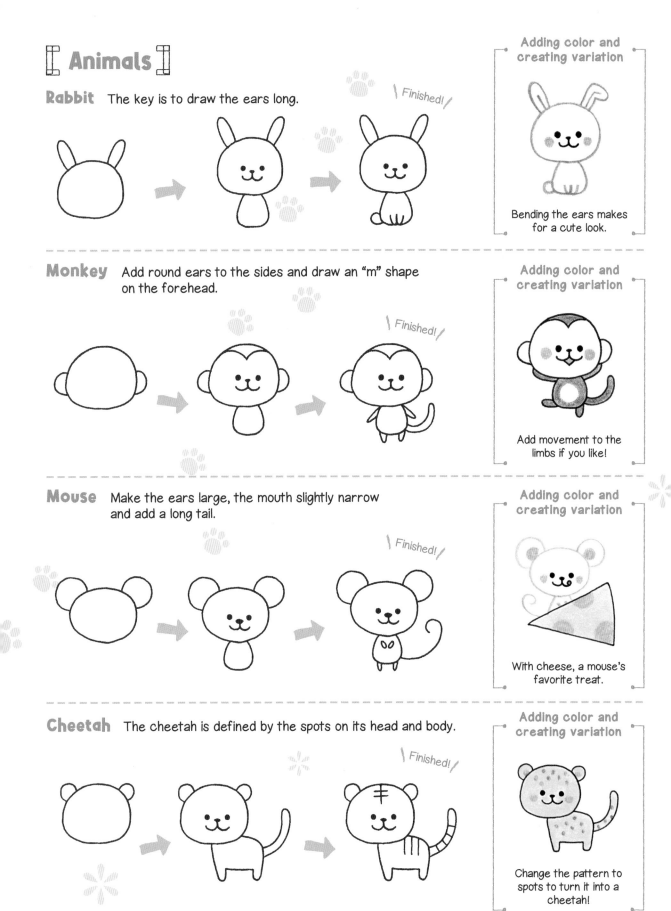

Bear   For large animals, make the body bulky.

\ Finished! /

Adding color and creating variation

Color the eyes, ears and limbs to make a panda.

Raccoon dog   The key is to draw the line around the eyes.

\ Finished! /

Adding color and creating variation

A tanuki (raccoon dog) beating his tummy.

Fox   Make the mouth slightly pointed. Draw fluffy fur around the neck.

\ Finished! /

Adding color and creating variation

Place a leaf on the head for a fox spirit that can change form.

Squirrel   The trick is to draw pointy ears and a large, rounded tail.

\ Finished! /

Adding color and creating variation

Add an acorn for a playful look.

Lion Emphasize the magnificent mane surrounding the face.

\ Finished! /

Adding color and creating variation

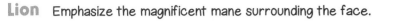

Add a crown as befits the king of beasts!

Koala The large nose is its defining feature, although the ears are large too.

\ Finished! /

Adding color and creating variation

Relaxing in a eucalyptus tree.

Pig The squashed snout is key. Square off the feet to indicate hooves.

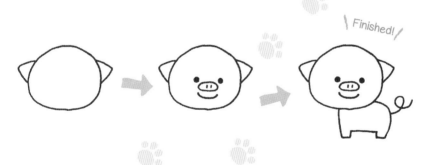

\ Finished! /

Adding color and creating variation

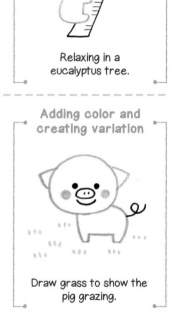

Draw grass to show the pig grazing.

Elephant Draw the trunk out from the circle, taking care with the initial shape.

\ Finished! /

Adding color and creating variation

Elephant playing with water in a puddle.

Sheep Draw curly wool on the forehead and around the entire body.

\ Finished! /

Adding color and creating variation

Close the eyes and add stars for a sleeping sheep.

Giraffe Make the neck long. The horn and markings are key.

\ Finished! /

Adding color and creating variation

Use yellow for the whole body with orange markings.

Horse Make the neck short, to accentuate the mane.

\ Finished! /

Adding color and creating variation

Add a pattern for a carousel horse!

● When it's tricky to draw the body......

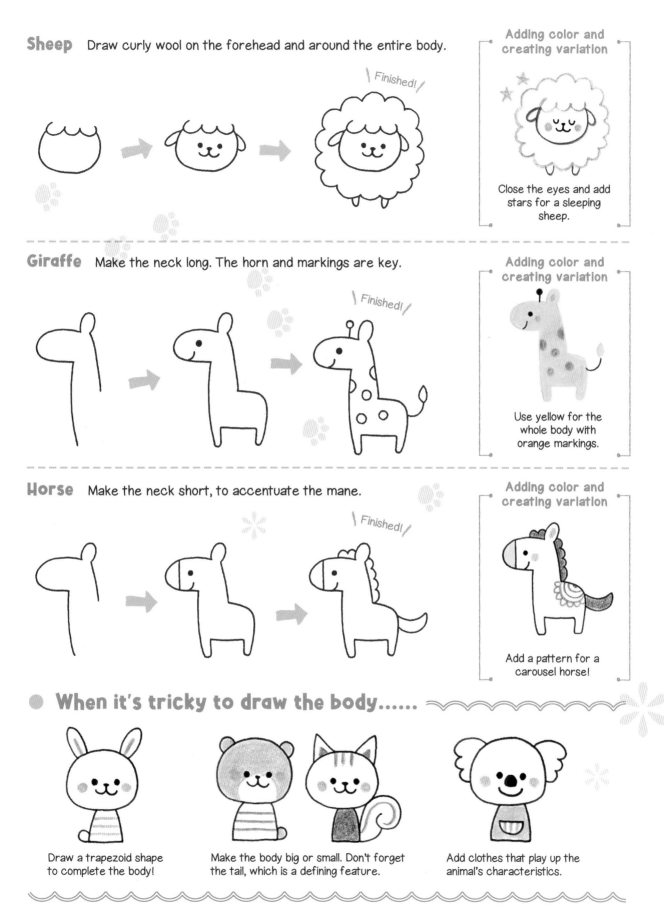

Draw a trapezoid shape to complete the body!

Make the body big or small. Don't forget the tail, which is a defining feature.

Add clothes that play up the animal's characteristics.

35

〖 Birds 〗

Bird (front view)

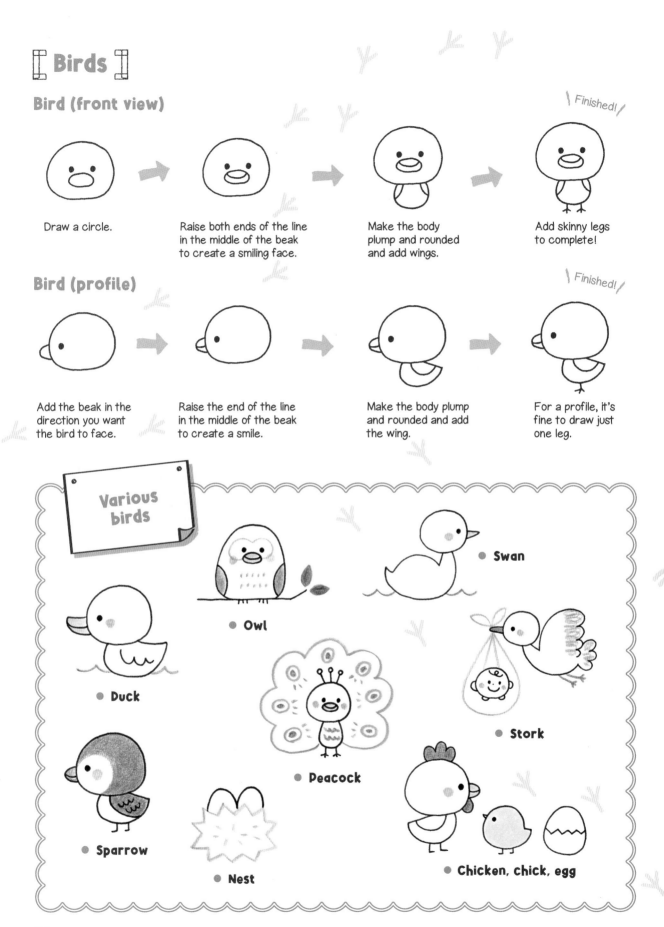

Draw a circle.

Raise both ends of the line in the middle of the beak to create a smiling face.

Make the body plump and rounded and add wings.

Add skinny legs to complete!

\ Finished! /

Bird (profile)

Add the beak in the direction you want the bird to face.

Raise the end of the line in the middle of the beak to create a smile.

Make the body plump and rounded and add the wing.

For a profile, it's fine to draw just one leg.

\ Finished! /

Various birds

● Swan

● Owl

● Duck

● Stork

● Peacock

● Sparrow

● Nest

● Chicken, chick, egg

⟦ Marine creatures ⟧

Fish   Draw an almond shape and add a triangle for a tail.

\ Finished! /

Adding color and creating variation

Try changing the size of the body or the color.

Whale   Creating a large, rounded back is key.

\ Finished! /

Adding color and creating variation

Spouting water while swimming.

Dolphin   Lengthen the snout and don't forget to add the dorsal fin.

\ Finished! /

Adding color and creating variation

Splashing and jumping in the water!

Tortoise   Draw a large lattice to create markings.

\ Finished! /

Adding color and creating variation

Add a sweatband to indicate effort.

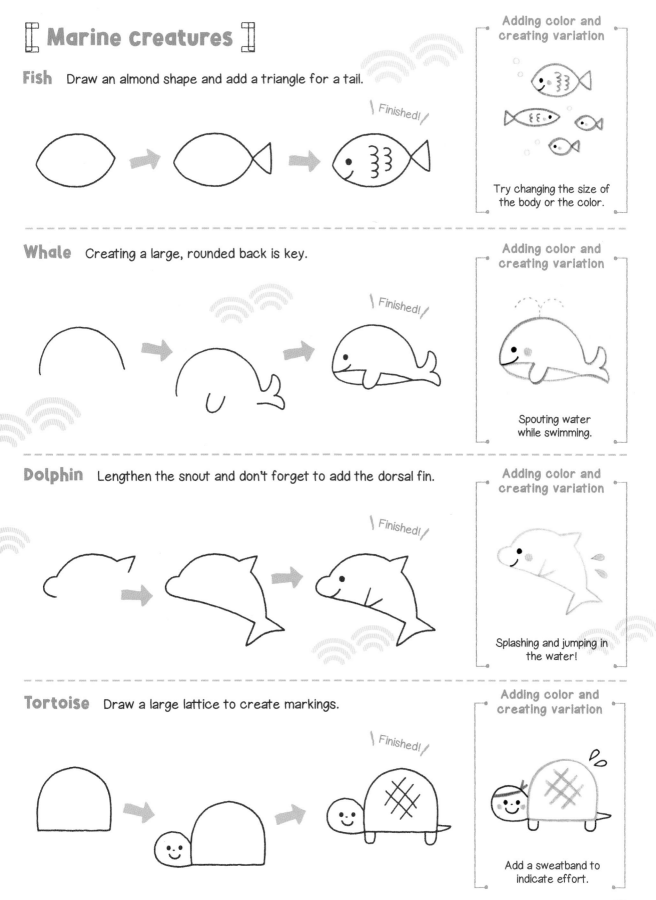

Penguin The face is the same as the bird (p.36). Make the figure chubby with short wings.

\ Finished! /

(p.36)

Adding color and creating variation

Color the head and wings blue and draw the penguin standing on the ice.

Seal The lolling body and short front legs are defining features.

\ Finished! /

Adding color and creating variation

Add snowflakes to convey a polar region.

Various marine creatures

● **Squid**
* Don't worry about drawing all 10 legs!

● **Shell**

● **Shrimp**

● **Sea anemone**

● **Octopus**

● **Fur seal**

● **Seaweed**

● **Jellyfish**

● **Shark**

⟦ Fantastic creatures ⟧

Unicorn Draw a horn onto a horse (p.35) and lengthen the mane.

\ Finished! /

Adding color and creating variation

Use fanciful colors for a striking result.

Monster Draw a giraffe (p.35) with a rounded back and thickened legs.

\ Finished! /

Adding color and creating variation

Add things like volcanoes for impact!

Dragon Draw a long facial outline. The whiskers and undulating body are key.

\ Finished! /

Adding color and creating variation

Drawing in clouds creates the sense of being in the sky.

Mermaid Draw the upper body as for a woman and the lower part as for a fish.

\ Finished! /

Adding color and creating variation

Add bubbles to make it look as if she is in the water.

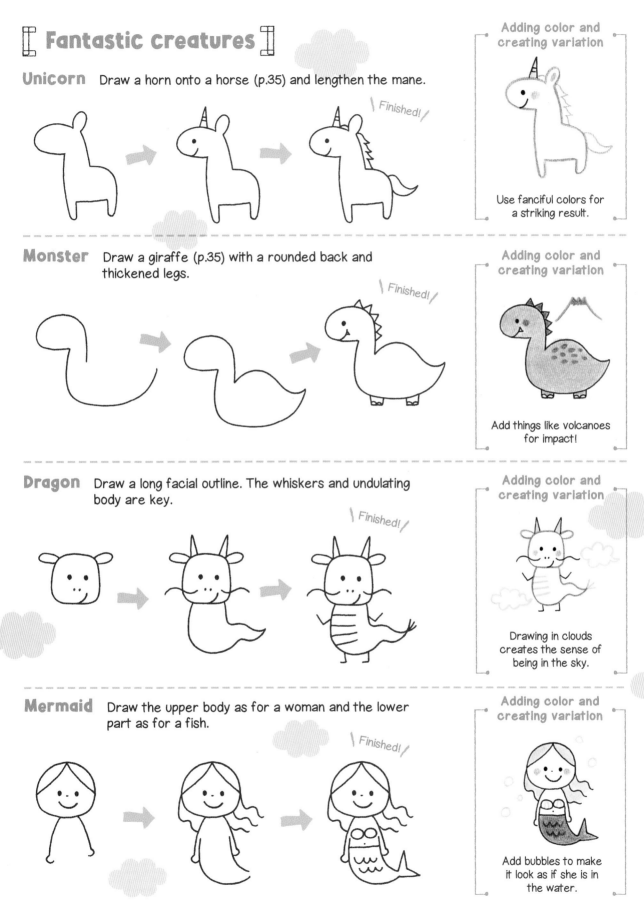

39

Basic Flowers and Trees

It's easy to draw cute flowers and trees.
Make them colorful and bright.

Flower 1

Draw the top petal.

Petals on both sides.

Left and right petals at the bottom.

Draw the stem and add leaves to complete!

\ Finished! /

Flower 2

Draw a circle.

Draw petals at the points of a cross.

Add petals in the gaps.

Draw the stem and add leaves to complete!

\ Finished! /

Tree 1

Draw a circle.

Add a trunk to complete!

\ Finished! /

Tree 2

Draw a lumpy outline.

Add a trunk to complete!

\ Finished! /

Tree 3

Draw a triangle.

Add the trunk.

Finished!

Draw branches to complete!

Adding color and creating variation

Make a winter tree by drawing only the trunk and branches.

Various flowers and trees

● Leaves

● Bouquet

● Vase

● Flower bed

● Fall colors

● Apple tree

● Flower pot

● Snow

Attendance Notebooks and Stickers

A handmade attendance notebook and stickers make for a school day to look forward to.

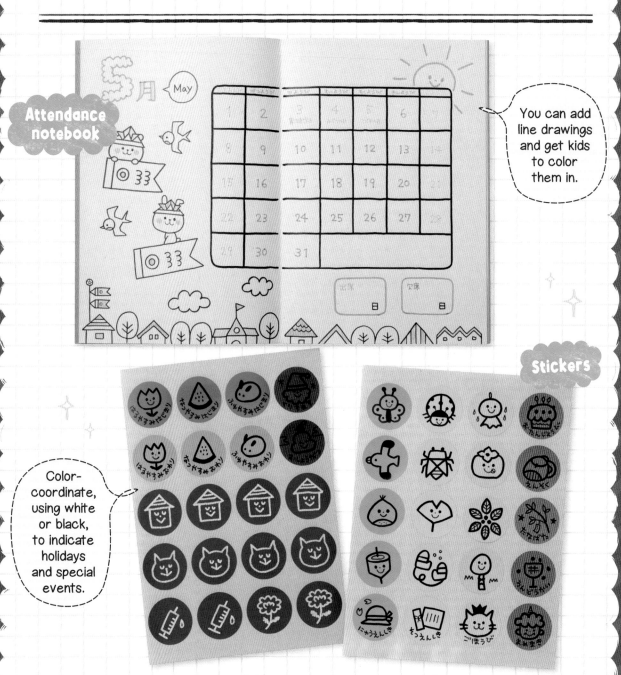

Attendance notebook

You can add line drawings and get kids to color them in.

Stickers

Color-coordinate, using white or black, to indicate holidays and special events.

Attendance notebook   sunny = p.28, cloudy = p.28, rabbit = p.32, bear = p.33, helmet = p.60, carp banner = p.60, tree = p.40-41, school = p.56
Stickers/left   tulip = p.57, watermelon = p.70, snow bunny = p.50, santa claus = p.88, ceremonial rice cakes = p.44, cat = p.30, injection = p.96
Stickers/right   butterfly = p.59, ladybug = p.62, weather charm = p.64, birthday cake = p.102, seagull = p.69, cicada = p.74, persimmon = p.77, backpack = p.61, chestnut = p.82, ginkgo leaf = p.84, poinsettia = p.89, bamboo and wish notes = p.68, top = p.44, mittens = 49, horsetail shoot = p.54, ball-toss game = p.81, hat = p.114, diploma = p.53, cat = p.30, ogre = p.48

PART TWO

Let's Draw Illustrations for the Twelve Months of the Year

There are all sorts of fun items and events associated with the school year, holidays and the seasons. From spring blossoms to a silly Santa, let's draw our way through the year with these adorable illustrations.

January

The year starts with New Year's Day. Use festive illustrations to capture the spirit of hope and newness.

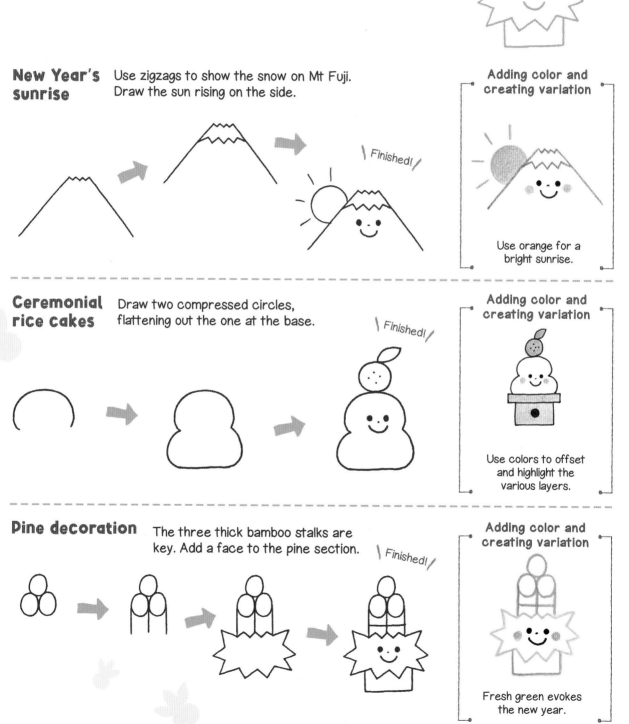

New Year's sunrise

Use zigzags to show the snow on Mt Fuji. Draw the sun rising on the side.

\ Finished! /

Adding color and creating variation

Use orange for a bright sunrise.

Ceremonial rice cakes

Draw two compressed circles, flattening out the one at the base.

\ Finished! /

Adding color and creating variation

Use colors to offset and highlight the various layers.

Pine decoration

The three thick bamboo stalks are key. Add a face to the pine section.

\ Finished! /

Adding color and creating variation

Fresh green evokes the new year.

Kite   Make the legs of the kite flutter so it appears to be flying in the wind.

\ Finished! /

Adding color and creating variation

Add a seasonal picture or image.

Paddle   Create a gradual tapering on the top section of the paddle.

\ Finished! /

Adding color and creating variation

Add movement effect lines to indicate a game in progress.

Top   Making the axis pass through the very center of the top is key.

\ Finished! /

Adding color and creating variation

Add a string to create the look of the top spinning.

Karuta game   Draw three rectangles, then draw the grabbing card,

\ Finished! /

New Year

Adding color and creating variation

New Year

Use green, purple, navy and other festive hues.

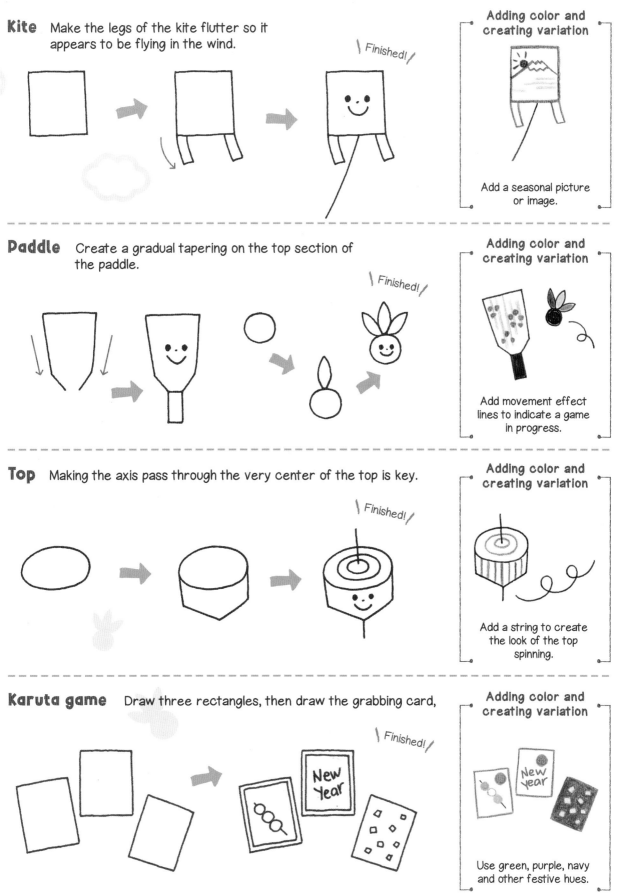

New Year's gift   Draw a ribbon in the middle of a rectangle.

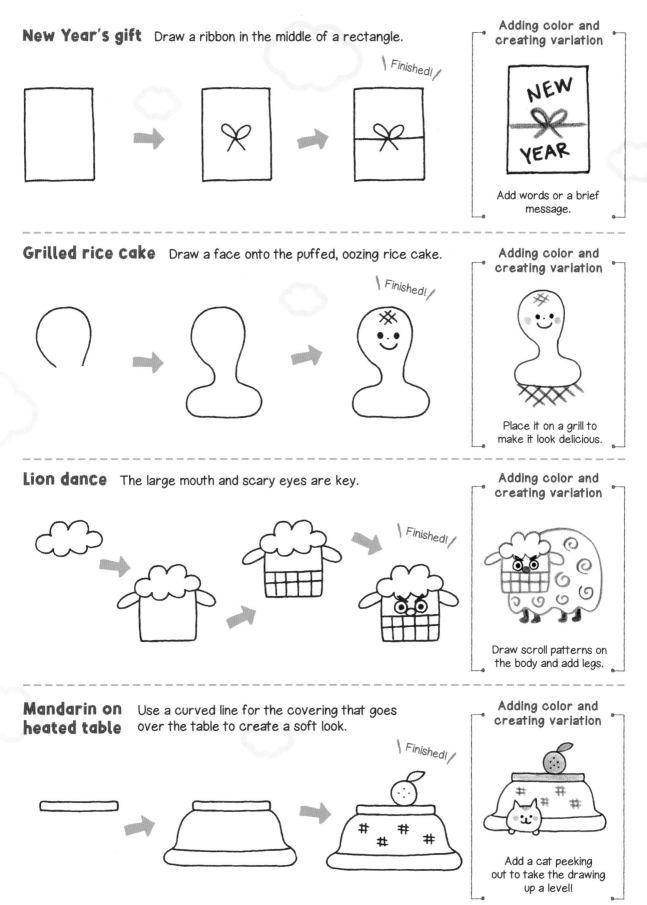

Finished!

Adding color and creating variation

NEW YEAR

Add words or a brief message.

Grilled rice cake   Draw a face onto the puffed, oozing rice cake.

Finished!

Adding color and creating variation

Place it on a grill to make it look delicious.

Lion dance   The large mouth and scary eyes are key.

Finished!

Adding color and creating variation

Draw scroll patterns on the body and add legs.

Mandarin on heated table   Use a curved line for the covering that goes over the table to create a soft look.

Finished!

Adding color and creating variation

Add a cat peeking out to take the drawing up a level!

46

1st of JANUARY

Baby's First Birthday

Out with the OLD In with the NEW

HAPPY NEW YEAR   HAPPY NEW YEAR

Rat

Ox

Tiger

Rabbit

Dragon

Snake

Horse

Sheep

Monkey

Rooster

Dog

Boar

H N Y

Let's Ring in the NEW YEAR

February

It's the month for Valentine's Day and winter fun. Layer on the warm clothing and make sure not to catch a cold!

Ogre
Draw curly hair, add fangs to the mouth and horns to the head.

\ Finished! /

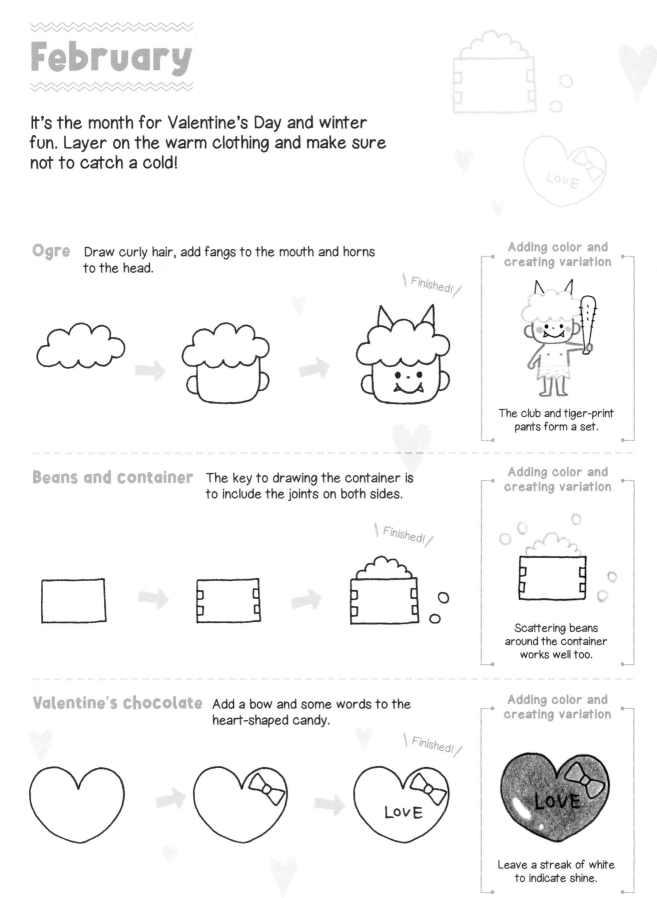

Adding color and creating variation

The club and tiger-print pants form a set.

Beans and container
The key to drawing the container is to include the joints on both sides.

\ Finished! /

Adding color and creating variation

Scattering beans around the container works well too.

Valentine's chocolate
Add a bow and some words to the heart-shaped candy.

\ Finished! /

LOVE

Adding color and creating variation

LOVE

Leave a streak of white to indicate shine.

Mittens and scarf
Make sure the hands are symmetrical for a charmingly balanced look.

\ Finished! /

\ Finished! /

Adding color and creating variation

Use the same color and patterns on both to create a set!

Winter clothing
Round out the lines to express the thickness of the coat.

\ Finished! /

Adding color and creating variation

Using a warm color adds warmth on a cold day.

Doctor
The white coat and stethoscope are key.

\ Finished! /

Adding color and creating variation

Coloring in the face makes the white coat stand out.

Mask
Make the mask large for emphasis. Don't forget the elastic that goes over the ears.

\ Finished! /

Adding color and creating variation

Use blue highlights to add detail.

Snow bunny The key here is to add ears and eyes to a dumpling shape.

\ Finished! /

Adding color and creating variation

Draw leaves for ears and berries for eyes.

Snowflake Make six equal lines that form the letter Y.

\ Finished! /

Adding color and creating variation

Make large and small snowflakes and add decorations.

Snow fort Draw one big dome then one small one and scatter snow all around.

\ Finished! /

Adding color and creating variation

Add an animal for dramatic effect!

Camellia The large stamens in the very center are the defining feature.

\ Finished! /

Adding color and creating variation

Make the leaves green and use red and white for the flower.

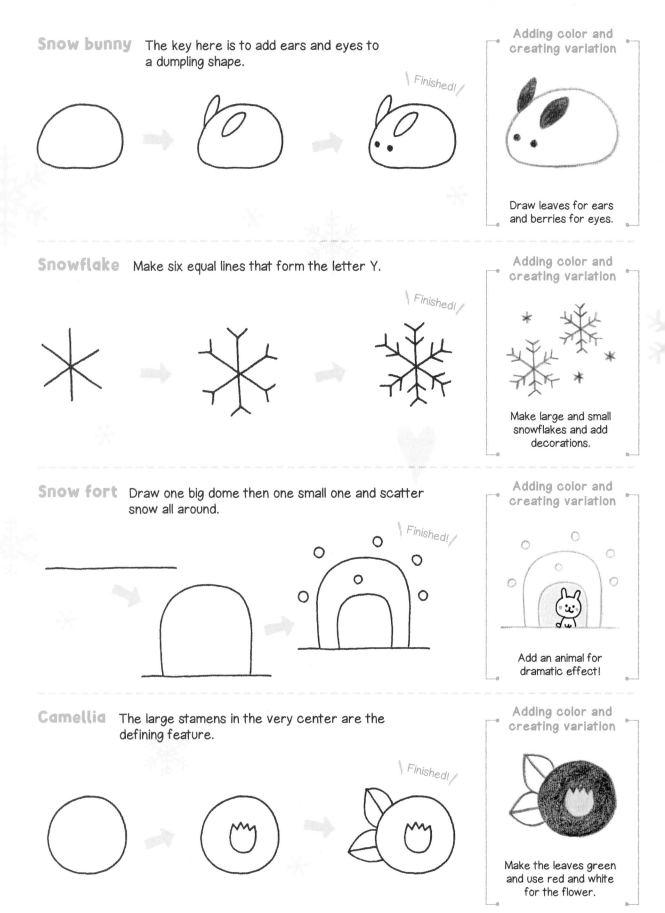

50

Spinach The trick is to draw large leaves that together form an inverted triangle.

\ Finished! /

Making the roots red is key.

Lotus root Draw a cylindrical shape and simply add holes.

\ Finished! /

Adding color and creating variation

Join two together and add a face if you like.

Combining illustrations and lettering

2 Hands Are Better Than One

28 Days
FEBRUARY

Be Mine

MASKS REQUIRED

While Supplies Last

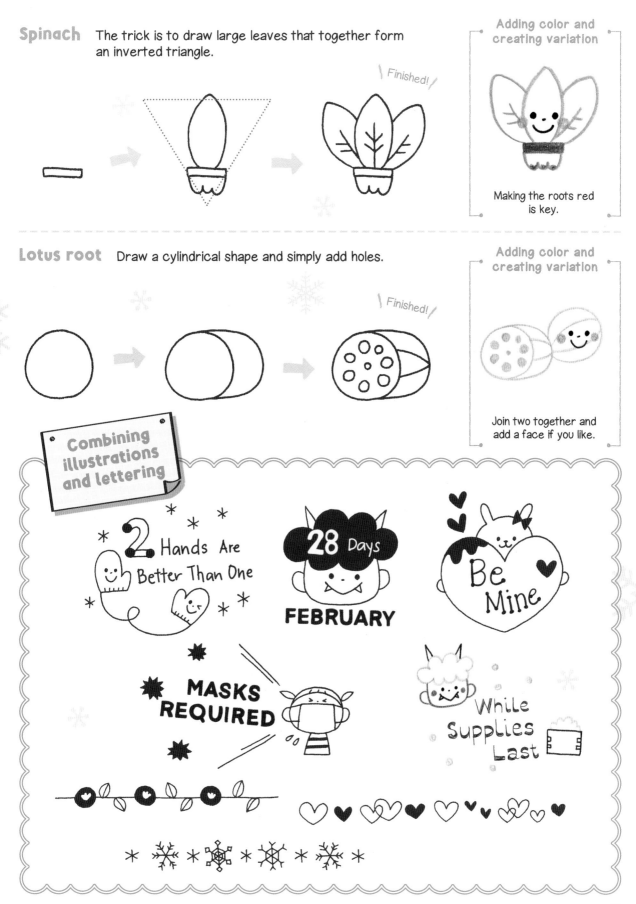

March

The blustery weather of the month brings hints of the warmer weeks ahead, while winter still reminds us it hasn't exited the scene yet.

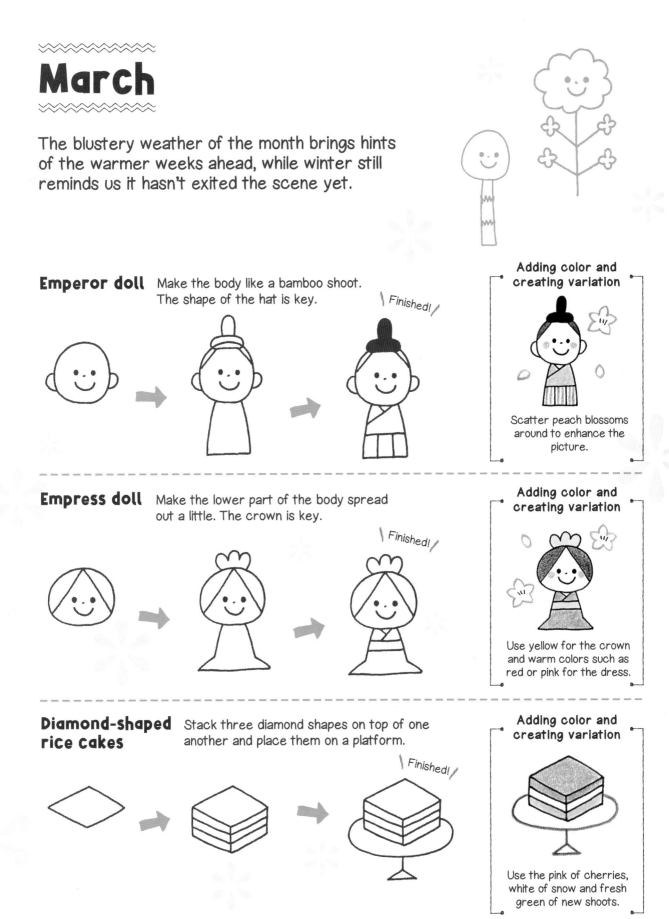

Emperor doll Make the body like a bamboo shoot. The shape of the hat is key.

\ Finished! /

Adding color and creating variation

Scatter peach blossoms around to enhance the picture.

Empress doll Make the lower part of the body spread out a little. The crown is key.

\ Finished! /

Adding color and creating variation

Use yellow for the crown and warm colors such as red or pink for the dress.

Diamond-shaped rice cakes Stack three diamond shapes on top of one another and place them on a platform.

\ Finished! /

Adding color and creating variation

Use the pink of cherries, white of snow and fresh green of new shoots.

Violet Make the lowest petal large and create a curve in the stem.

Finished!

Adding color and creating variation

Use blue or purple for the flower and green for the leaves.

Rapeseed flower Make a large cluster of little flowers, with two flowers on each side underneath.

Finished!

Adding color and creating variation

The combination of yellow and green creates a spring vibe.

Graduating student Use the uniform and scroll cylinder to create the look of a graduating pupil.

Finished!

Adding color and creating variation

Scatter cherry blossoms around for a spring feeling.

Diploma Draw the certificate and scroll as a set.

Finished!

Adding color and creating variation

Use yellow or gold on the certificate.

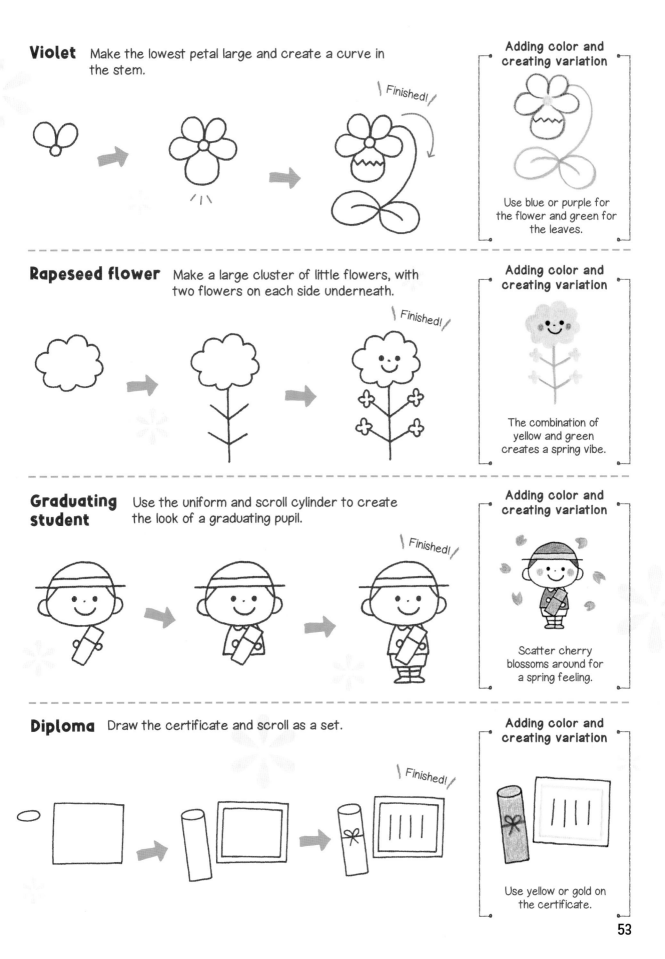

School bag   Making a bold curve in the flap of the bag is key.

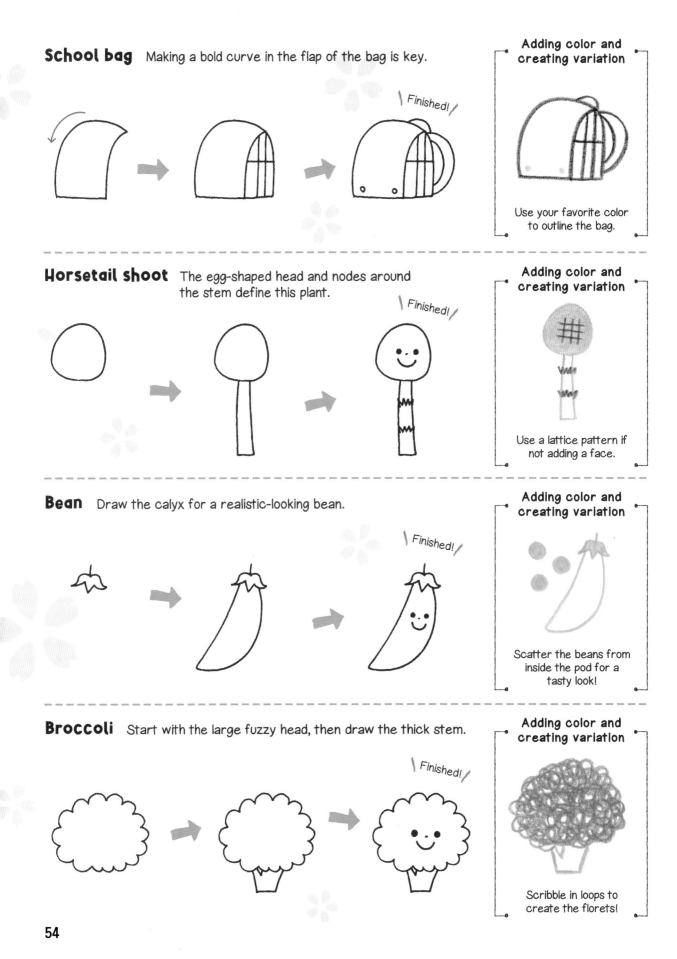

\ Finished! /

Adding color and creating variation

Use your favorite color to outline the bag.

Horsetail shoot   The egg-shaped head and nodes around the stem define this plant.

\ Finished! /

Adding color and creating variation

Use a lattice pattern if not adding a face.

Bean   Draw the calyx for a realistic-looking bean.

\ Finished! /

Adding color and creating variation

Scatter the beans from inside the pod for a tasty look!

Broccoli   Start with the large fuzzy head, then draw the thick stem.

\ Finished! /

Adding color and creating variation

Scribble in loops to create the florets!

3 MARCH
Madness

CRAFT SALE

CONGRATS GRADS

SCHOOL NEWS

I ♥ U

For You

Made with LOVE

55

April

This is the season of new growth, spring break and the mounting feeling of excitement at the warmer months ahead.

Student Draw a bag hanging over one shoulder and the legs and arms swinging boldly.

\ Finished! /

Adding color and creating variation

Use yellow and sky blue or other complementary hues.

Cherry blossoms Start drawing from the trunk. Make sure to split the petals.

\ Finished! /

Adding color and creating variation

Arrange five petals in a circle.

School Adding a flag and clock to the building with a triangular roof adds authenticity.

\ Finished! /

Adding color and creating variation

Clouds and flowers elevate the picture!

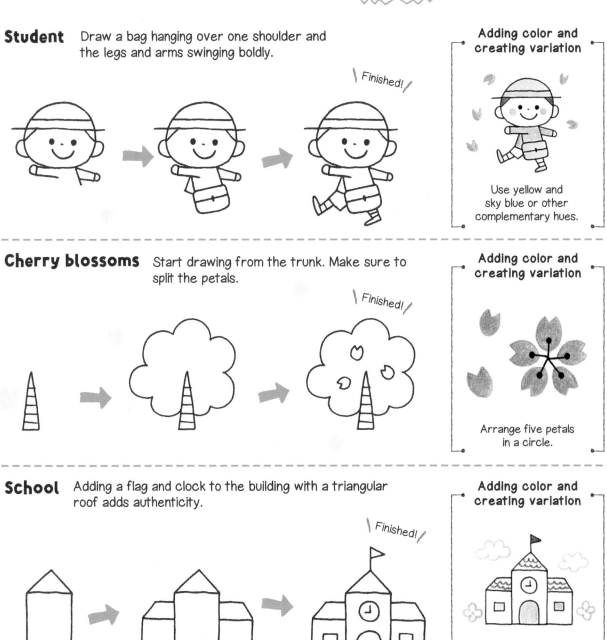

Tulip Drawing the long, slightly narrow leaves from the base of the stem is key.

A bowl-shaped bloom

\ Finished! /

For white flowers, just draw an outline.

Dandelion Create jagged leaves that spread out at the base of the stem.

\ Finished! /

Add flying, fluffy seeds for a fun look!

Fish Create a rounded belly and draw the eyes high on the head.

\ Finished! /

Draw bubbles to show the fish is in the water.

Clover Create heart-shaped indentations in the leaf tips.

\ Finished! /

Visualize a four-leaf clover

Closing the eyes adds variety to the drawing.

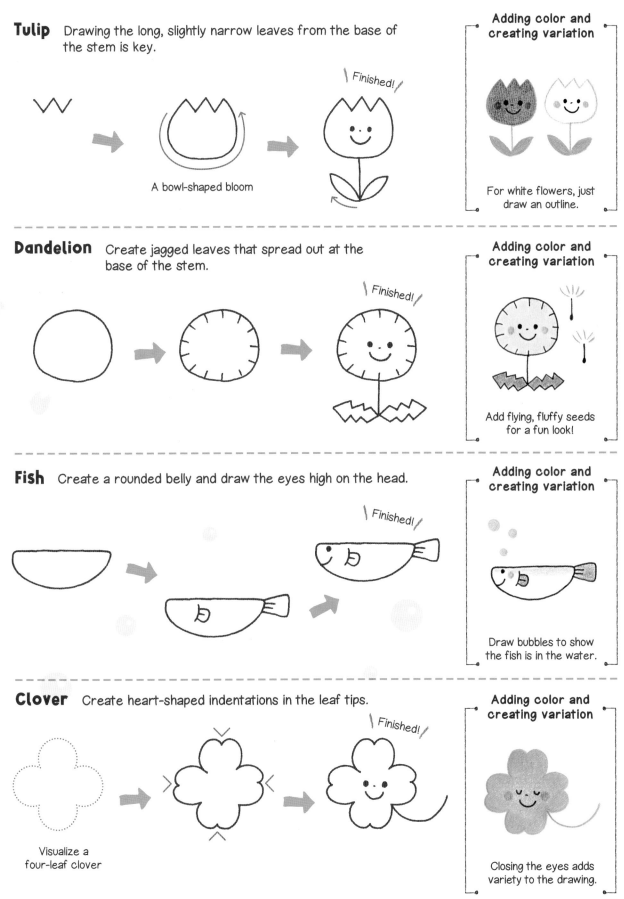

57

Health check

For both the scale and the height chart, drawing the increments is key.

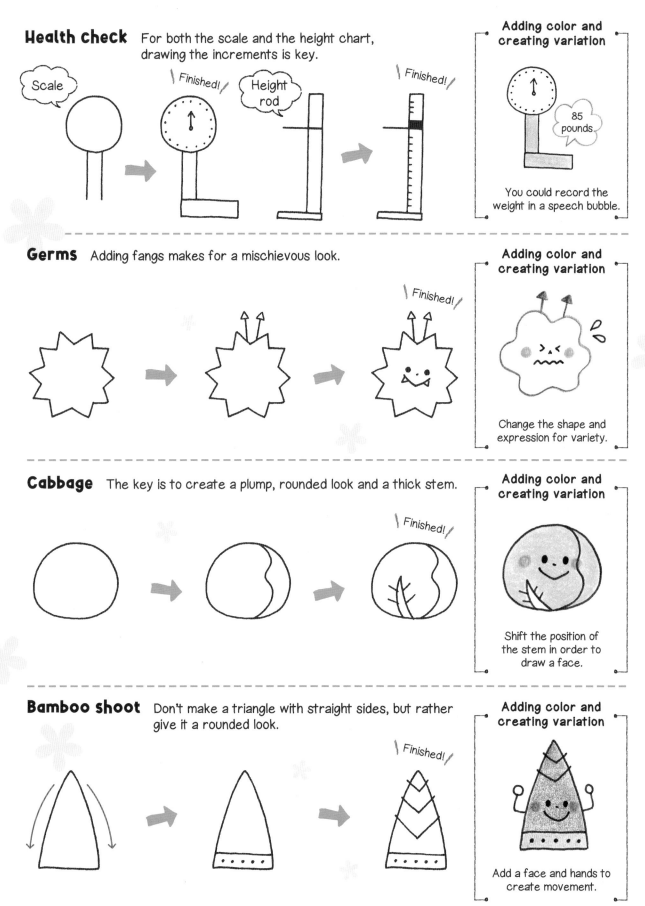

Scale

Finished!

Height rod

Finished!

Adding color and creating variation

85 pounds

You could record the weight in a speech bubble.

Germs

Adding fangs makes for a mischievous look.

Finished!

Adding color and creating variation

Change the shape and expression for variety.

Cabbage

The key is to create a plump, rounded look and a thick stem.

Finished!

Adding color and creating variation

Shift the position of the stem in order to draw a face.

Bamboo shoot

Don't make a triangle with straight sides, but rather give it a rounded look.

Finished!

Adding color and creating variation

Add a face and hands to create movement.

Butterfly   Rounding the wings creates a gentle, buoyant look.

\ Finished! /

Adding color and creating variation

Position the figure at an angle and add dots to make it appear to be flying.

Bee   The key is to make the end of the body pointed.

\ Finished! /

Adding color and creating variation

Show the bee carrying honey!

Combining illustrations and lettering

4 APRIL

4 APRIL FOOLS!

Health Fair

It's SPRING Break!

School's Closed

May

With Mother's Day, Cinco de Mayo and school trips, there's plenty happening in the fifth month, and plenty to draw!

Carp banner   Big eyes make for a lively expression.

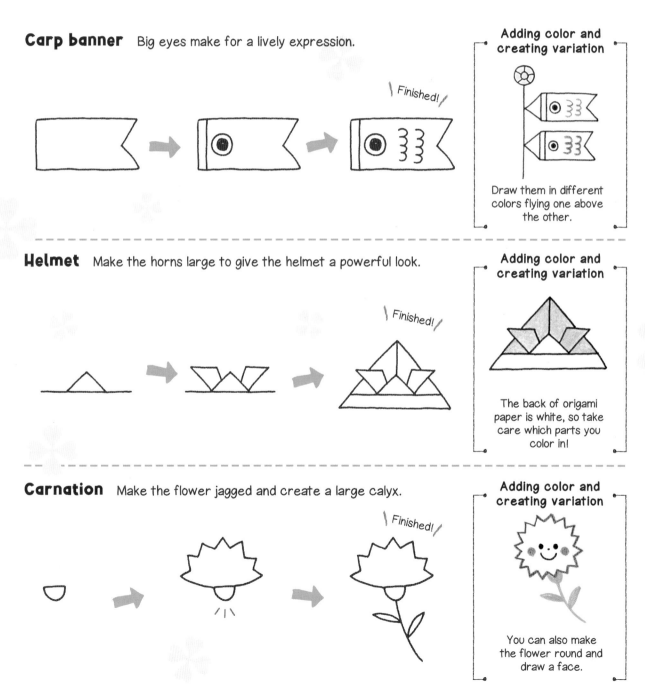

Finished!

Adding color and creating variation

Draw them in different colors flying one above the other.

Helmet   Make the horns large to give the helmet a powerful look.

Finished!

Adding color and creating variation

The back of origami paper is white, so take care which parts you color in!

Carnation   Make the flower jagged and create a large calyx.

Finished!

Adding color and creating variation

You can also make the flower round and draw a face.

Bus Draw a large windshield and several small windows.

\ Finished! /

Adding color and creating variation

Adding a bus stop is a nice touch.

Backpack Round out the lower section to give the bag shape and fullness.

\ Finished! /

Adding color and creating variation

Use different colors and patterns as decoration.

Combining illustrations and lettering

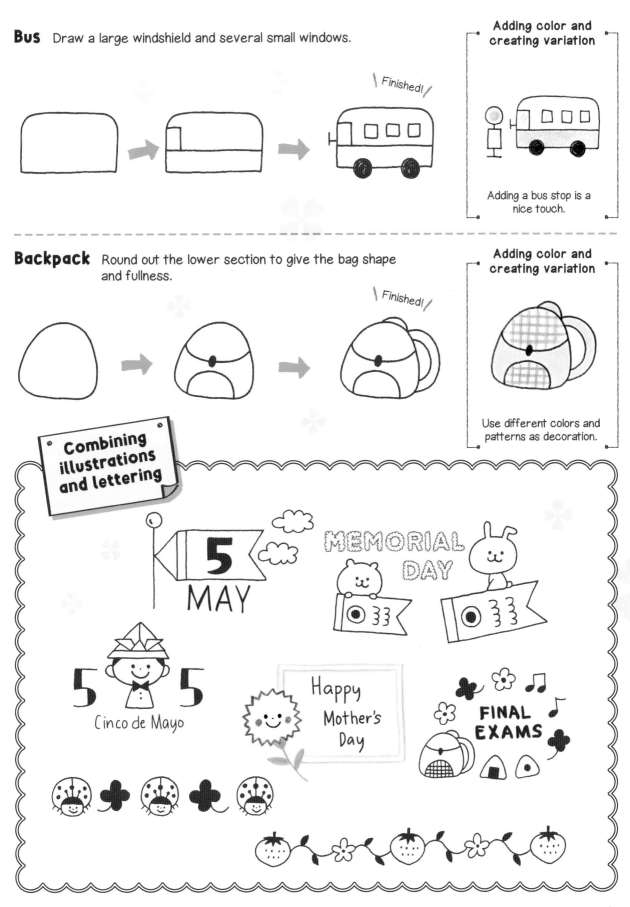

5 MAY

MEMORIAL DAY

5 5 Cinco de Mayo

Happy Mother's Day

FINAL EXAMS

Lunchbox   Choose colorful side dishes for a tasty meal.

Finished!

Adding color and creating variation

Add a drink bottle in the same color as the lunchbox for a cohesive look.

Caterpillar   Add stripes on the body to create a soft look.

Finished!

Adding color and creating variation

Add movement lines to the caterpillar's rear.

Ladybug   Create a large, round body for an adorable look.

Finished!

Adding color and creating variation

Ladybugs go well with clover.

Ant   Make the chest area small for a realistic effect.

Finished!

Adding color and creating variation

Draw three ants one after another marching in a line.

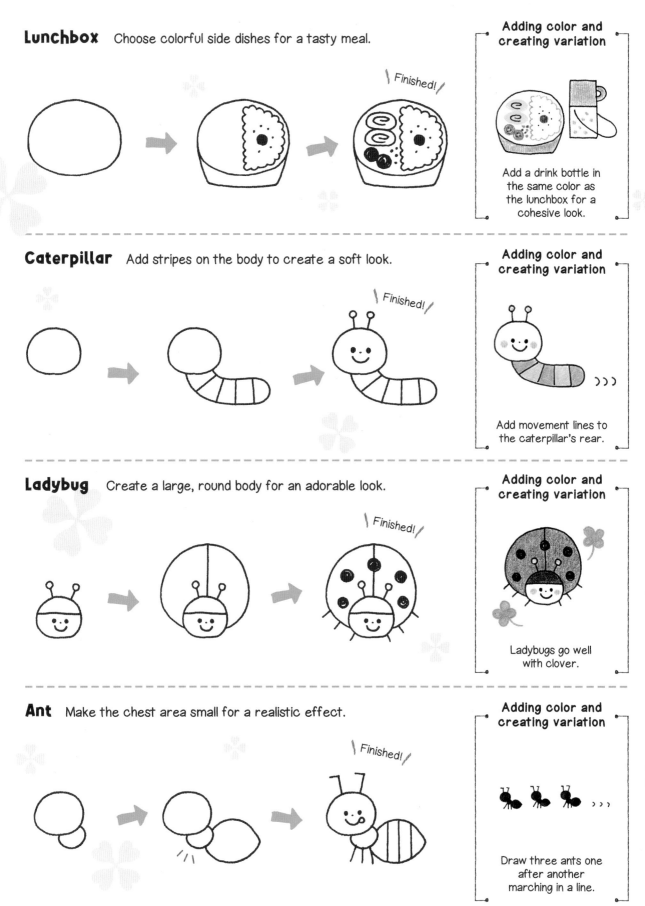

Strawberry Make the bottom of the fruit pointy and add a scattering of seeds.

Finished!

Adding color and creating variation

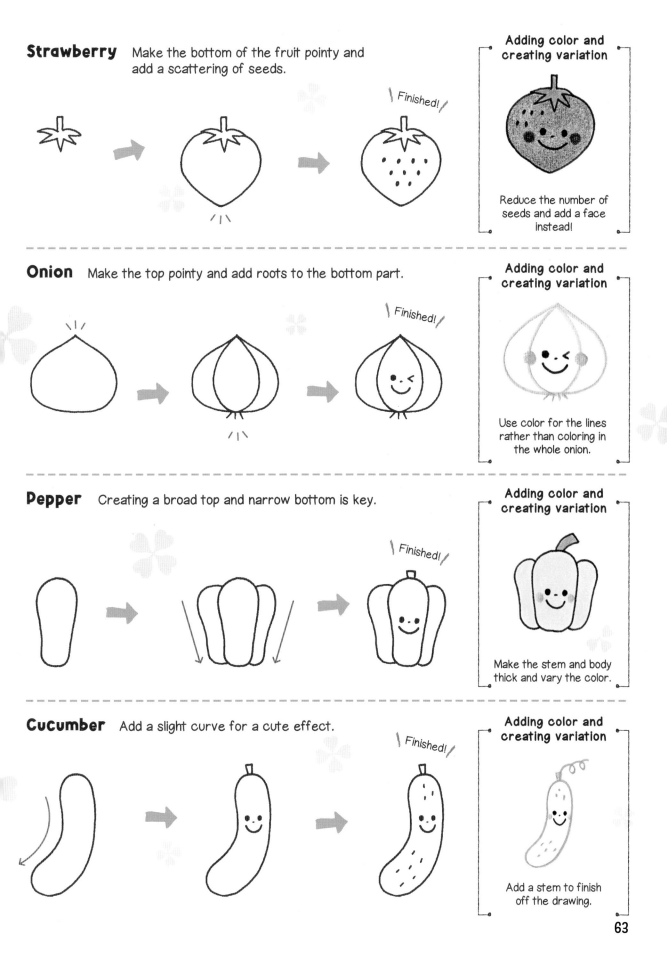

Reduce the number of seeds and add a face instead!

Onion Make the top pointy and add roots to the bottom part.

Finished!

Adding color and creating variation

Use color for the lines rather than coloring in the whole onion.

Pepper Creating a broad top and narrow bottom is key.

Finished!

Adding color and creating variation

Make the stem and body thick and vary the color.

Cucumber Add a slight curve for a cute effect.

Finished!

Adding color and creating variation

Add a stem to finish off the drawing.

June

There is a lot of rain at this time of year, marking the start of summer and the day set aside to celebrate fathers.

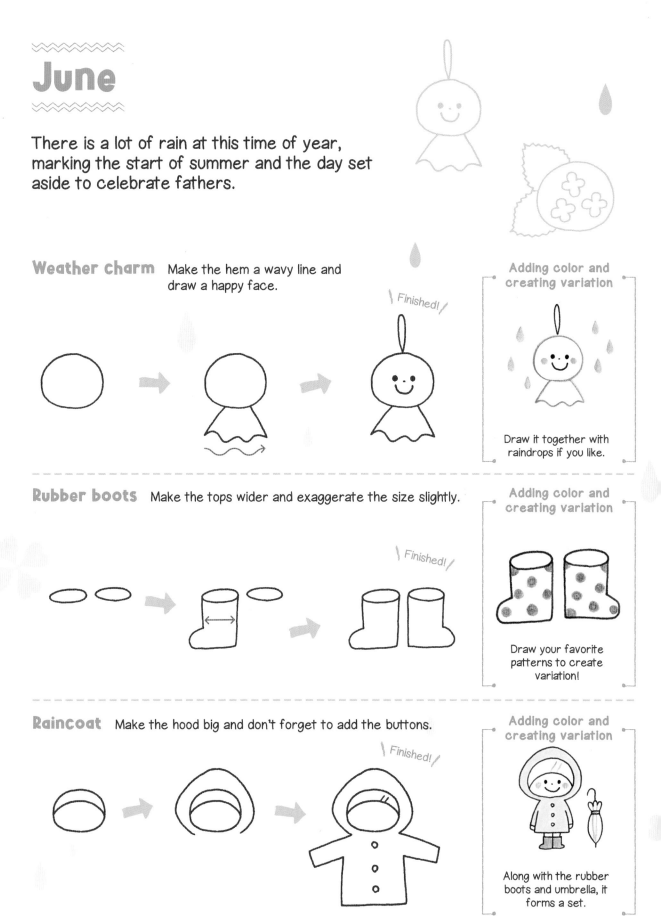

Weather charm
Make the hem a wavy line and draw a happy face.

\ Finished! /

Adding color and creating variation

Draw it together with raindrops if you like.

Rubber boots
Make the tops wider and exaggerate the size slightly.

\ Finished! /

Adding color and creating variation

Draw your favorite patterns to create variation!

Raincoat
Make the hood big and don't forget to add the buttons.

\ Finished! /

Adding color and creating variation

Along with the rubber boots and umbrella, it forms a set.

64

Rainbow   Rather than seven colors, keep things neat with just three.

\ Finished! /

Make the outer arch red and the inner arch blue.

Hydrangea   The key is to make the flower section round and the leaves large and jagged.

\ Finished! /

Adding color and creating variation

Add raindrops for a dramatic effect.

Frog   The protruding eyes and crablike legs are adorable.

\ Finished! /

Adding color and creating variation

Add a tail to a circle to create tadpoles.

Snail   Take care to balance the shell and the body.

\ Finished! /

Adding color and creating variation

Remove the shell to create a slug.

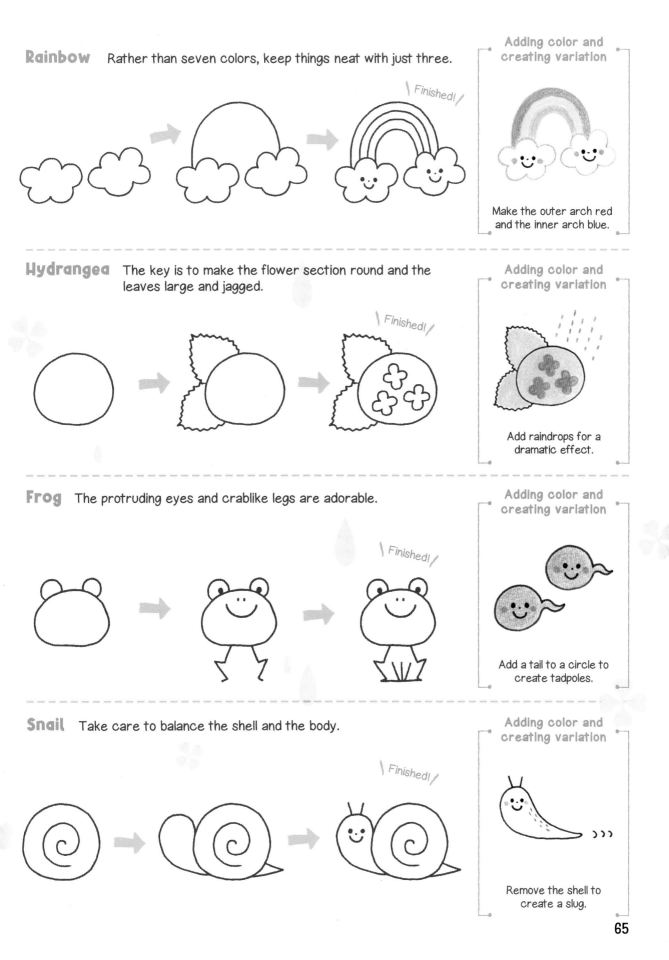

65

Brushing teeth

Make the mouth large and draw a lattice to form the teeth. Add a toothbrush and sparkly symbols.

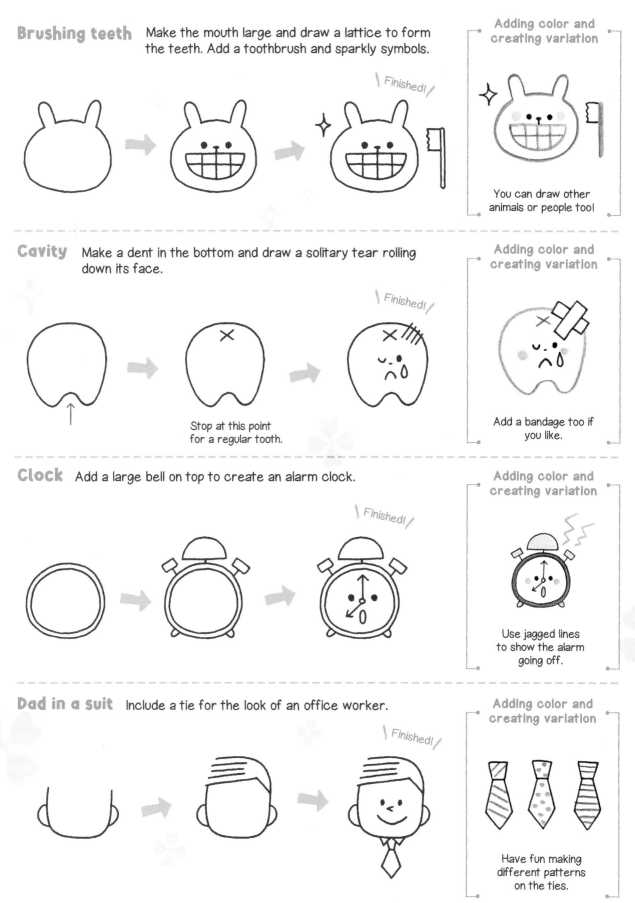

\ Finished! /

Adding color and creating variation

You can draw other animals or people too!

Cavity

Make a dent in the bottom and draw a solitary tear rolling down its face.

\ Finished! /

Stop at this point for a regular tooth.

Adding color and creating variation

Add a bandage too if you like.

Clock

Add a large bell on top to create an alarm clock.

\ Finished! /

Adding color and creating variation

Use jagged lines to show the alarm going off.

Dad in a suit

Include a tie for the look of an office worker.

\ Finished! /

Adding color and creating variation

Have fun making different patterns on the ties.

66

Melon When drawing the face, shift the lattice pattern to make room.

\ Finished! /

Adding color and creating variation

Draw a cross-section of melon like this.

Cherries Draw two circles together to create realistic cherries.

\ Finished! /

Adding color and creating variation

Make them pink or red or a combination.

Combining illustrations and lettering

6 JUNE

Trip to the Dentist

COOL CAT

HAPPY FATHER'S DAY

SPRING FLING JUNE 21st

Wake up!

July

Look to the night sky in July and you just might see fireworks! Fun times abound, whether it's cooling off at the seaside, eating frozen treats or gazing at stars.

Weaver girl star The double bun on her head is the key to drawing this character.

Finished!

Adding color and creating variation

Add a celestial robe for a more impressive look.

Cowherd boy star Draw a topknot or single bun on top of his head.

Finished!

Adding color and creating variation

Scatter stars around to complete the drawing.

Bamboo and wish notes Don't forget to create notches when drawing the bamboo.

Finished!

Adding color and creating variation

Create various ornaments and decorations.

Pool   Raising both hands makes for an active, energetic pose.

\ Finished! /

Adding color and creating variation

Draw lanes for a realistic look.

Sea   Fluffy clouds create a realistic seaside scene.

\ Finished! /

Adding color and creating variation

Draw in the sun and add some seagulls and waves.

Crab   Exaggerate the claws for a more comic effect.

\ Finished! /

Adding color and creating variation

Sand and seashells create a summery feel.

Seagull   Section off the ends of the wings to color them in.

\ Finished! /

Adding color and creating variation

Make them appear to be flying far away.

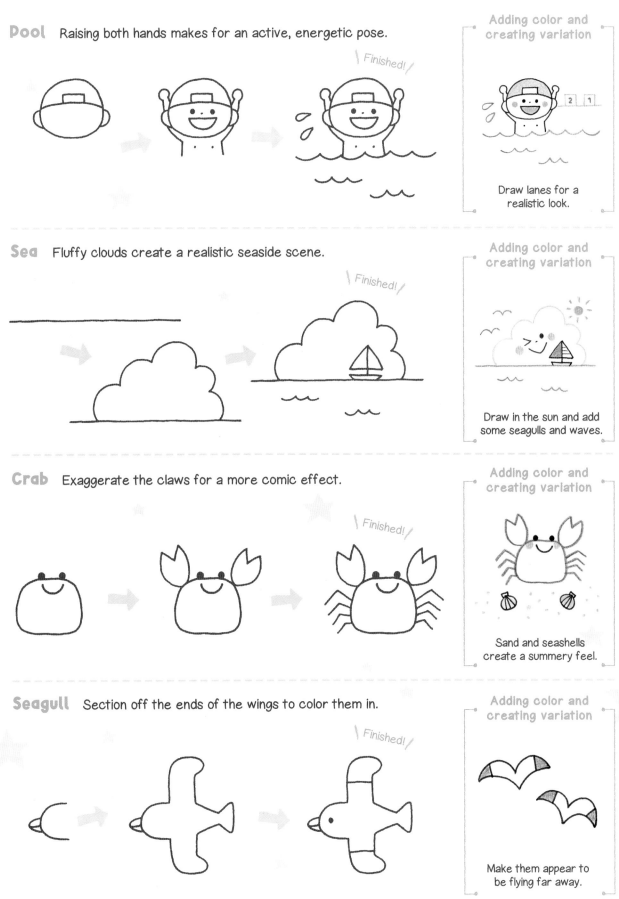

69

High noon Emphasize the cheeks to make the figure look hot.

Finished!

Adding color and creating variation

Draw in a roasting sun as well if you like.

Fan The key is to draw lines radiating out above the handle.

Finished!

Adding color and creating variation

Drawing fireworks heightens the sense of summer.

Watermelon The zigzag lines on the skin are a defining feature.

Finished!

Adding color and creating variation

Show various slices too. Don't forget the seeds.

Morning glory Make the flowers trumpet-shaped, adding vines and leaves.

Finished!

Adding color and creating variation

Make the flowers pink, purple or blue.

Corn When drawing a face, keep the kernels to a minimum.

\ Finished! /

If you're not adding a face, cover the whole surface with kernels.

Mosquito Adding a drop of blood at the end of the pointed stinger makes it clear that this is a mosquito.

\ Finished! /

Add a line behind the bottom to show the mosquito in flight.

Combining illustrations and lettering

7 JULY

BEACH Week

Vacation Itinerary

Fourth of JULY

BANG

POOL PARTY

August

Fruits and vegetables are at their peak, and this is the last month of summer freedom to pursue those warm-weather hobbies.

Sunflower Open the mouth wide for a cheerful appearance.

\ Finished! /

Adding color and creating variation

If not adding a face, use a lattice pattern instead.

Fireworks Start drawing from the center with the shapes getting gradually larger.

\ Finished! /

Adding color and creating variation

Increasing the number of shapes makes for a gorgeous effect.

Shaved ice Use straight lines for the ice and curved lines for the syrup.

\ Finished! /

Adding color and creating variation

Use blues to convey the cool ice.

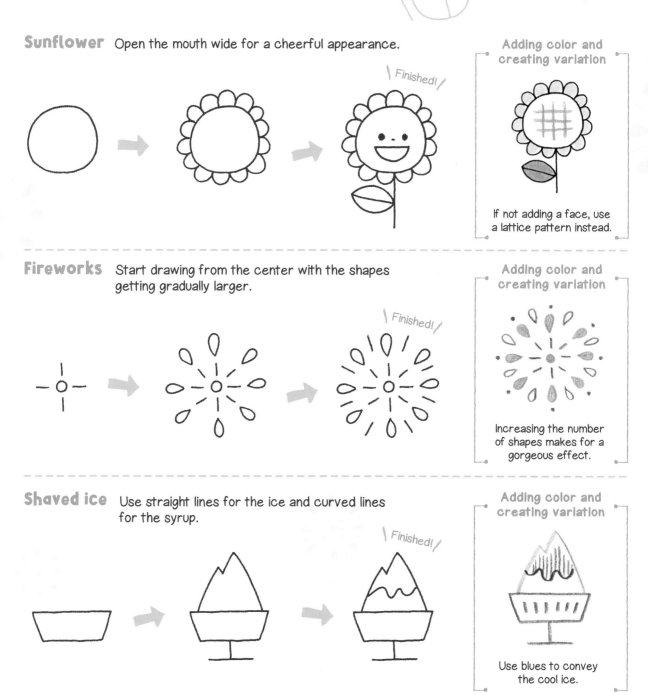

Peach Make sure the top comes to a point and add a line at the base.

\ Finished! /

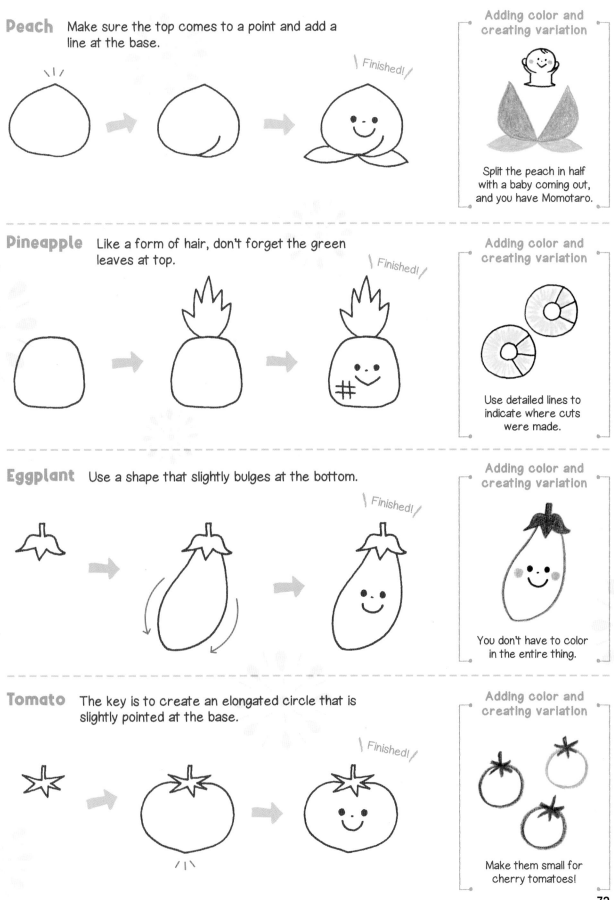

Adding color and creating variation

Split the peach in half with a baby coming out, and you have Momotaro.

Pineapple Like a form of hair, don't forget the green leaves at top.

\ Finished! /

Adding color and creating variation

Use detailed lines to indicate where cuts were made.

Eggplant Use a shape that slightly bulges at the bottom.

\ Finished! /

Adding color and creating variation

You don't have to color in the entire thing.

Tomato The key is to create an elongated circle that is slightly pointed at the base.

\ Finished! /

Adding color and creating variation

Make them small for cherry tomatoes!

73

Bugcatcher   Use a lattice pattern for the cage and the net.

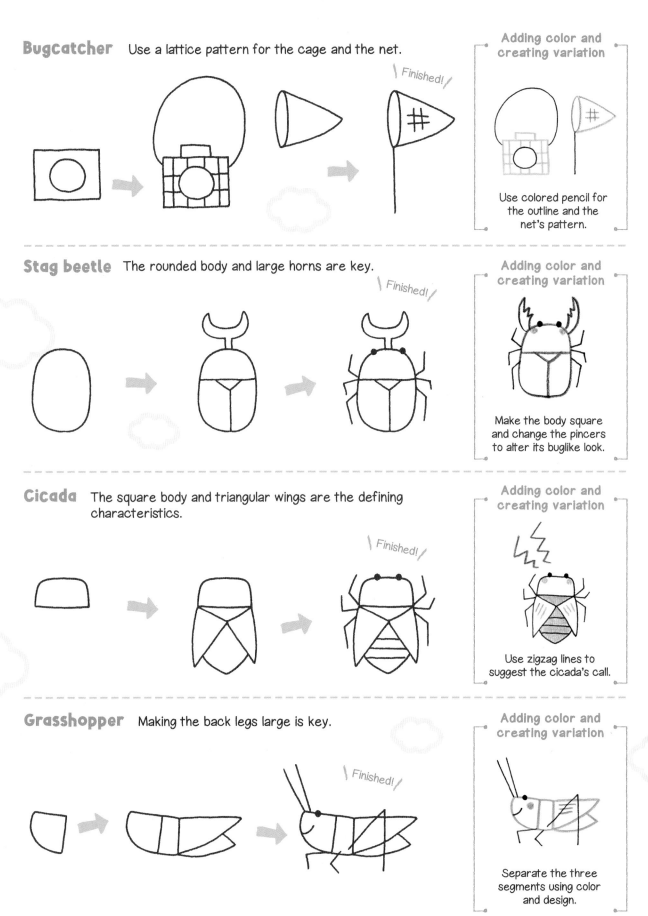

\ Finished! /

Adding color and creating variation

Use colored pencil for the outline and the net's pattern.

Stag beetle   The rounded body and large horns are key.

\ Finished! /

Adding color and creating variation

Make the body square and change the pincers to alter its buglike look.

Cicada   The square body and triangular wings are the defining characteristics.

\ Finished! /

Adding color and creating variation

Use zigzag lines to suggest the cicada's call.

Grasshopper   Making the back legs large is key.

\ Finished! /

Adding color and creating variation

Separate the three segments using color and design.

Palm tree Make the leaves long and outstretched and the trunk supple.

\ Finished! /

Adding color and creating variation

Draw the sea in the background for a tropical feel.

Firefly Draw sparks of light coming from the insect's bottom.

\ Finished! /

Adding color and creating variation

Draw large circles of light to indicate a swarm.

Combining illustrations and lettering

8 AUGUST

8 AUGUST
. . . .
NEWSLETTER

H 2 O
Stay Hydrated!!

FRESH Produce

LAZY DAYS

September

Time to get ready for the long fall nights ahead. There's a coolness in the air and the last gasps of summer, as the leaves prepare to change hues.

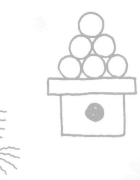

Moon viewing   Stack the dumplings to form a pyramid.

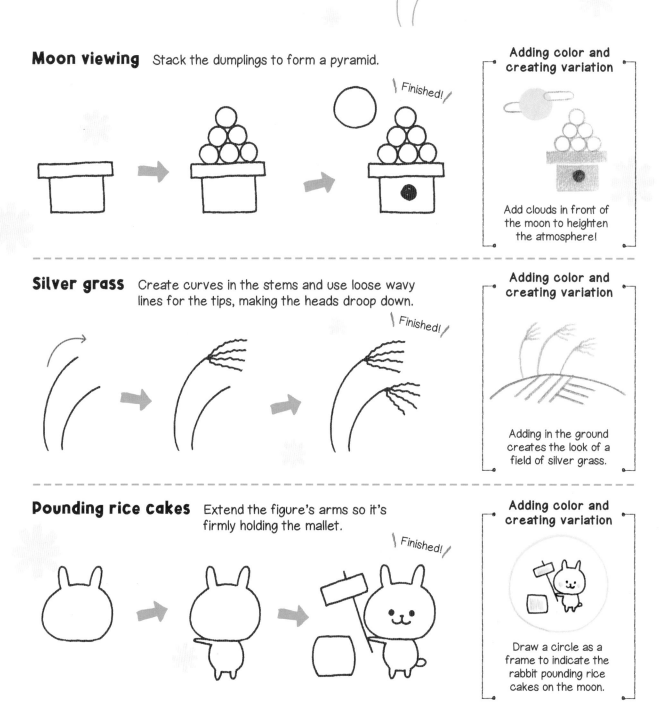

Finished!

Adding color and creating variation

Add clouds in front of the moon to heighten the atmosphere!

Silver grass   Create curves in the stems and use loose wavy lines for the tips, making the heads droop down.

Finished!

Adding color and creating variation

Adding in the ground creates the look of a field of silver grass.

Pounding rice cakes   Extend the figure's arms so it's firmly holding the mallet.

Finished!

Adding color and creating variation

Draw a circle as a frame to indicate the rabbit pounding rice cakes on the moon.

Cosmos There are eight petals. Create a cross to position the petals so they're equally spaced.

Finished!

Use pink or red for the flower.

Grapes The key is to draw with an inverted triangle in mind.

Finished!

Use purple to draw the fruit for a realistic look.

Persimmon The shape of the calyx is important. For the fruit, picture a square as you draw.

Finished!

Using green for the calyx creates a nice contrast.

Banana Draw a bunch of about three bananas for a well-balanced look.

Finished!

A peeled banana looks like this.

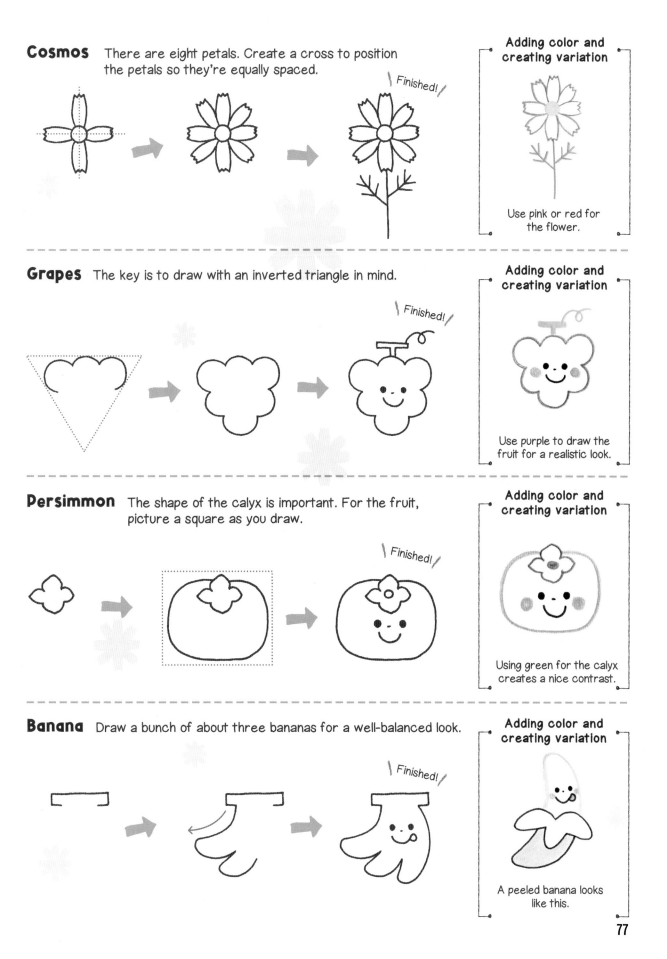

Hood   Make the top of the hood slightly pointed.

Finished!

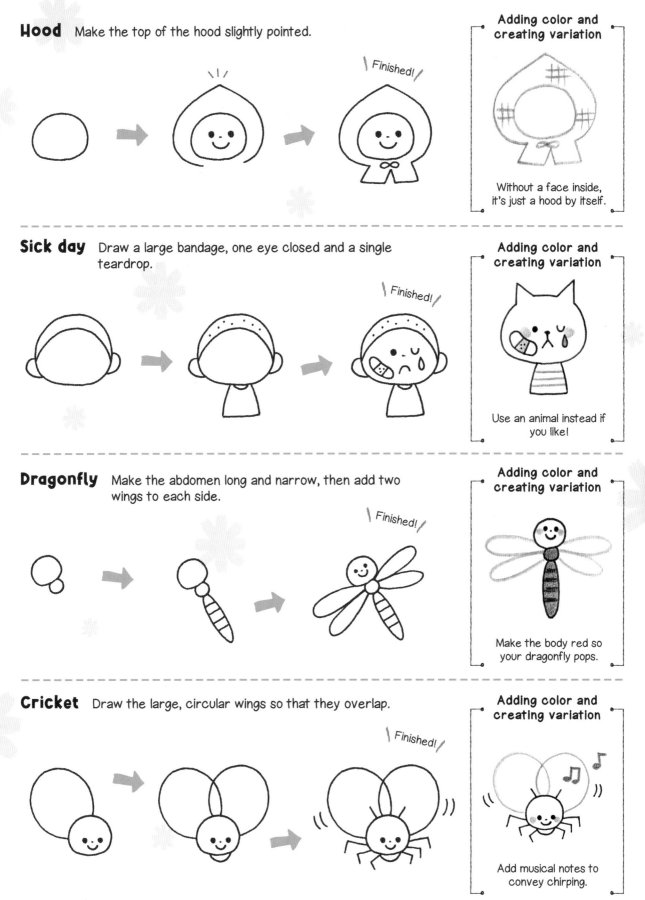

Adding color and creating variation

Without a face inside, it's just a hood by itself.

Sick day   Draw a large bandage, one eye closed and a single teardrop.

Finished!

Adding color and creating variation

Use an animal instead if you like!

Dragonfly   Make the abdomen long and narrow, then add two wings to each side.

Finished!

Adding color and creating variation

Make the body red so your dragonfly pops.

Cricket   Draw the large, circular wings so that they overlap.

Finished!

Adding color and creating variation

Add musical notes to convey chirping.

October

Boo! The spooky fun of Halloween is just around the corner, but so are harvest festivals and fall sporting events.

National flags   Choose flags that are easily recognizable.

\ Finished! /

Adding color and creating variation

Combine various national flags for a good result.

Running a race   The key is to make the finishing-line tape big and wide.

\ Finished! /

Adding color and creating variation

WINNER!!

Draw letters inside the tape if you like.

Medal   Make the ribbon wide for a cute effect.

\ Finished! /

Adding color and creating variation

Add sparkle symbols to show luster and shine.

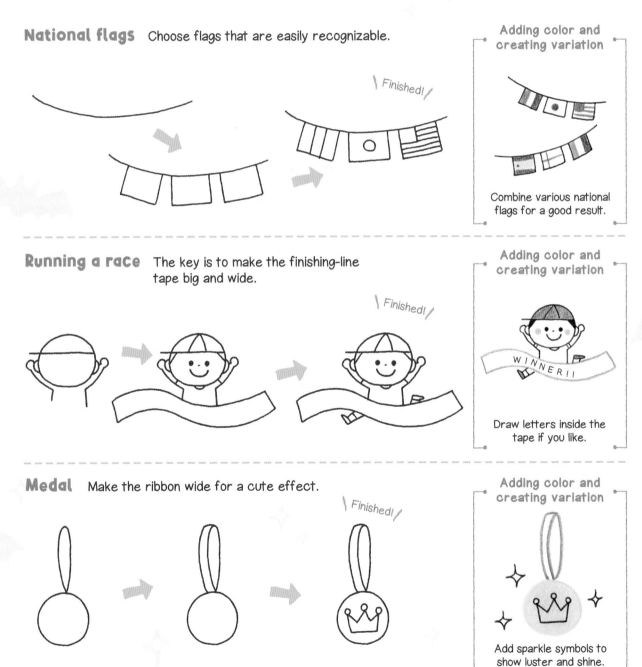

Ball-toss game Draw the balls outside the basket as well as inside to create a sense of movement.

\ Finished! /

Try using different colors for the balls.

Ghost Use wavy lines for the hem. Including legs adds a comic effect.

Adding color and creating variation

\ Finished! /

Add a triangular hat for a witchy, Halloween vibe

Bat Creating peaks in the upper sections of the wings is key.

Adding color and creating variation

\ Finished! /

Draw the bats in silhouette with stars around them.

Witch Slightly bend the tip of the hat and make the hair stringy.

Adding color and creating variation

\ Finished! /

Add a broom to complete the character!

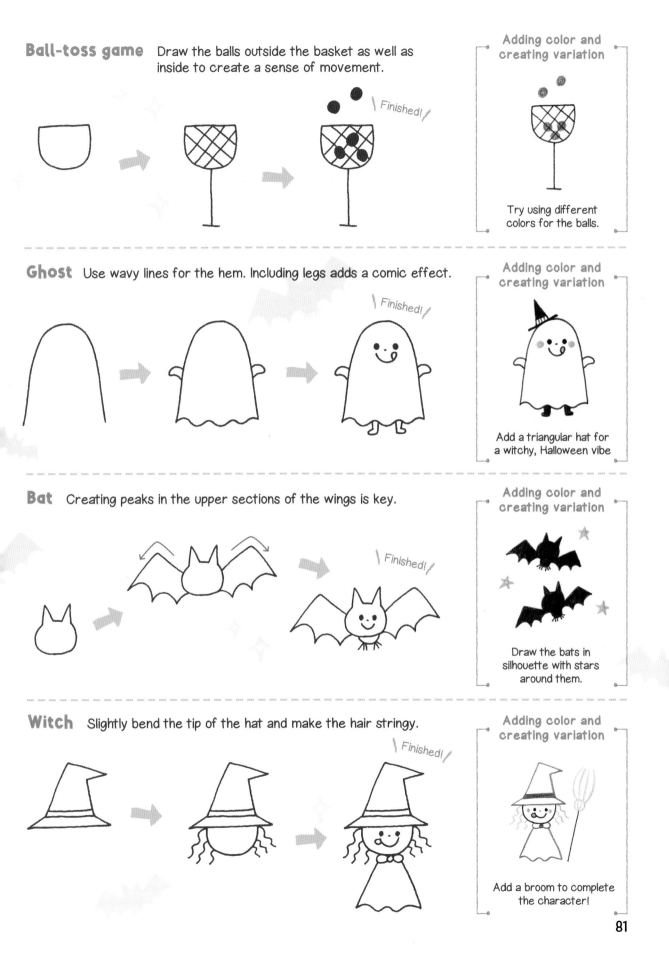

Acorn For the head, draw a semi-circle with a line coming out of the center.

\ Finished! /

Adding color and creating variation

Draw small acorns and add lines to create the appearance of motion.

Chestnut Make the base wide and the top pointed.

\ Finished! /

Adding color and creating variation

Add the casing behind it to create a background.

Sweet potato Create a swollen center with tapered ends.

\ Finished! /

Adding color and creating variation

Color the cross-sections yellow and add steam.

Pumpkin The key is to create three rounded peaks, then add a stem and vine.

\ Finished! /

Adding color and creating variation

Add fangs for a Halloween effect.

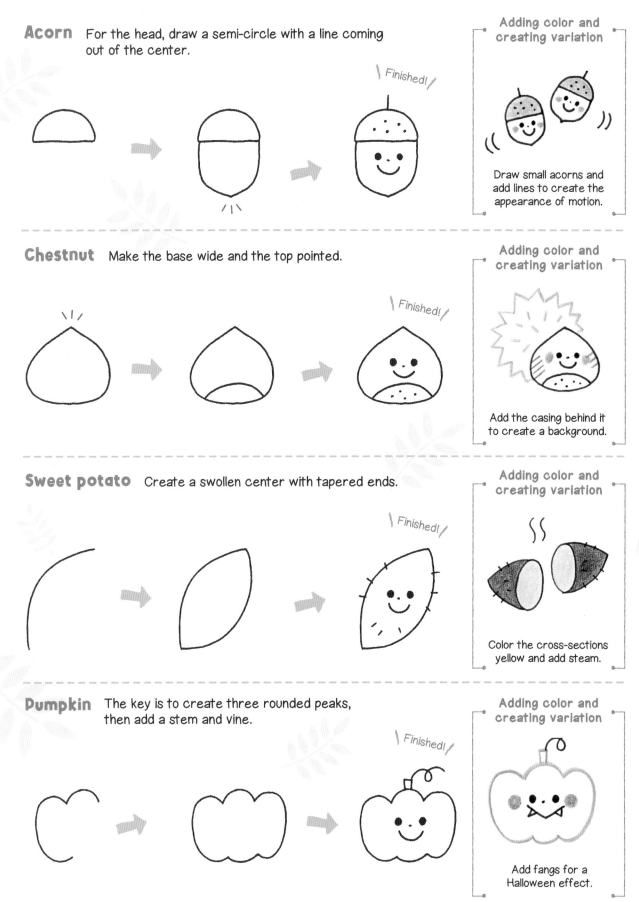

Carrot & daikon radish

Give the carrot a tapered tip but make the daikon pointed.

Finished!

Finished!

Adding color and creating variation

Show the differences in the leaves too.

Combining illustrations and lettering

10 Boo! OCTOBER

CULTURE FAIR

RACE DAY

Let's Go Leaf Peeping

TRICK OR TREAT

HALLO WEEN

Nature CLUB

November

Falling leaves, the bountiful feast of Thanksgiving and the first hints of winter mean November is upon us.

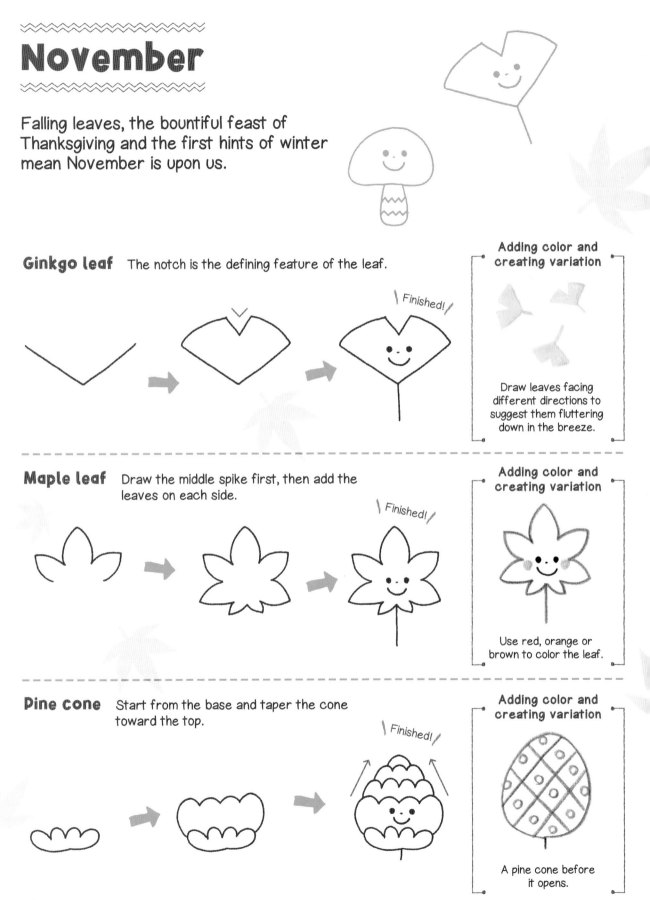

Ginkgo leaf   The notch is the defining feature of the leaf.

\ Finished! /

Adding color and creating variation

Draw leaves facing different directions to suggest them fluttering down in the breeze.

Maple leaf   Draw the middle spike first, then add the leaves on each side.

\ Finished! /

Adding color and creating variation

Use red, orange or brown to color the leaf.

Pine cone   Start from the base and taper the cone toward the top.

\ Finished! /

Adding color and creating variation

A pine cone before it opens.

Cocoon Draw an upside-down triangle to capture the slim, tapered shape.

Finished!

Add a branch for a realistic look.

Reading Draw an open book with a glimpse of the head and both hands behind it.

Finished!

BOOK

You can print letters onto the book too.

Drum Place drumsticks on a cylinder to create a drum.

Finished!

Add musical notes for a fun, colorful look.

Piano The curve on the right side is key.

Finished!

Scatter different colored musical notes all around.

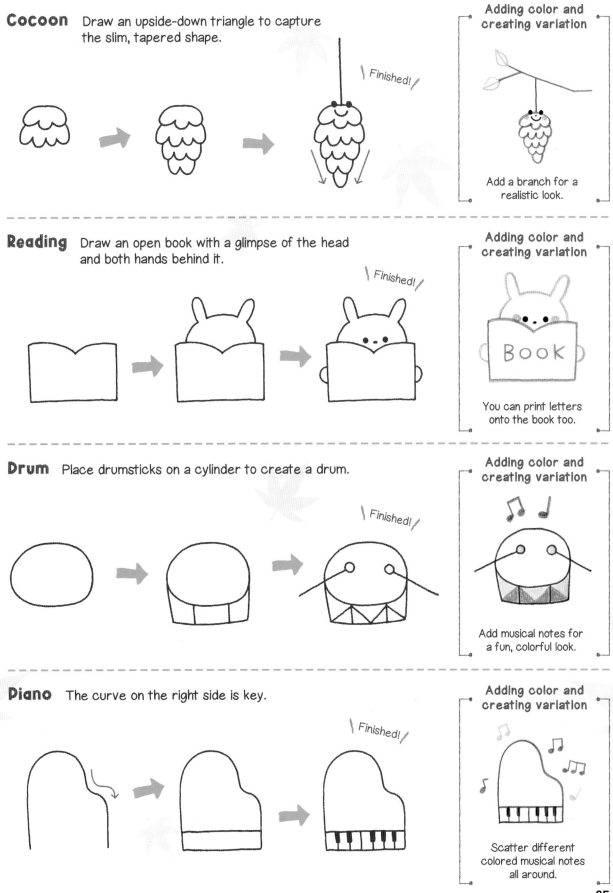

Festival
To make a sign, draw a nature scene on a long rectangle and add text.

\ Finished! /

Adding color and creating variation

Add balloons to amplify the festive air.

Paint
Make the tube slightly broader at the base.

\ Finished! /

Adding color and creating variation

Have the figure hold a brush and draw a drop of paint.
*Squirrel → p.33

Apple
Make a slight dent in the top and add a stem and leaves.

\ Finished! /

Adding color and creating variation

For a cross-section, draw one seed.

Mushroom
Make the entire shape rounded for an accurate effect.

\ Finished! /

Adding color and creating variation

Alter the cap and stem to create different types of mushrooms.

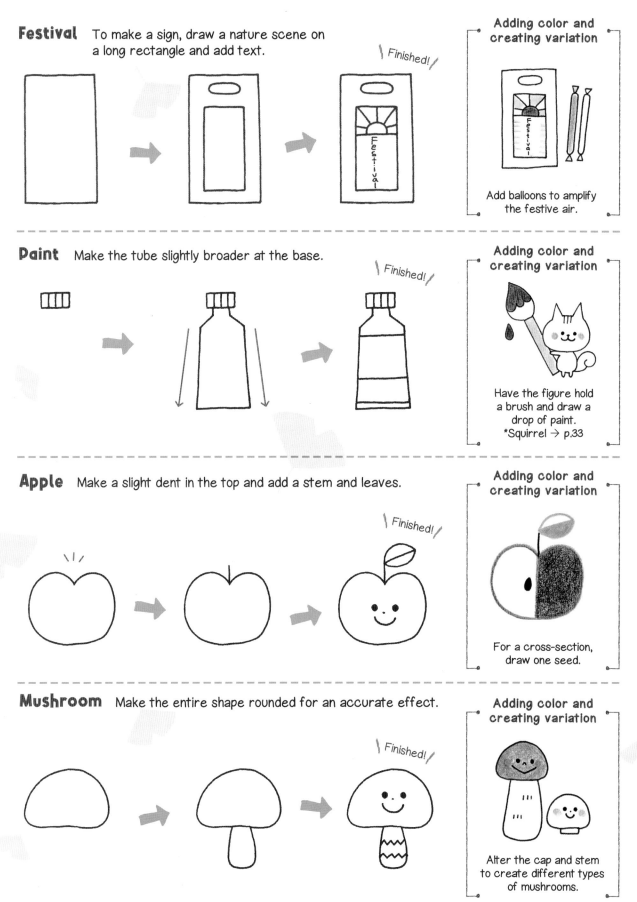

December

The year is drawing to a close, so pull on your warm layers and get ready for the festivities and fun of December.

Christmas tree   Draw about three triangles on top of one another.

\ Finished! /

Adding color and creating variation

Use the traditional Christmas colors red and green.

Santa Claus   A big, full beard adds the right fun and festive tone.

\ Finished! /

Adding color and creating variation

Use the classic red for Santa's costume.

Reindeer   Large, splendid antlers and a red nose are the defining characteristics.

\ Finished! /

Adding color and creating variation

Leave a circular patch of the nose uncolored to indicate shine.

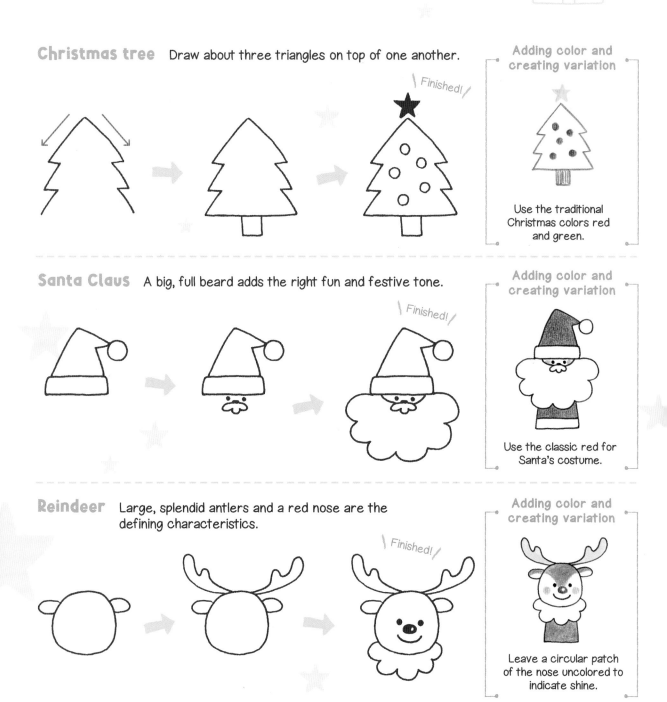

Present Draw a bow and add a square to complete.

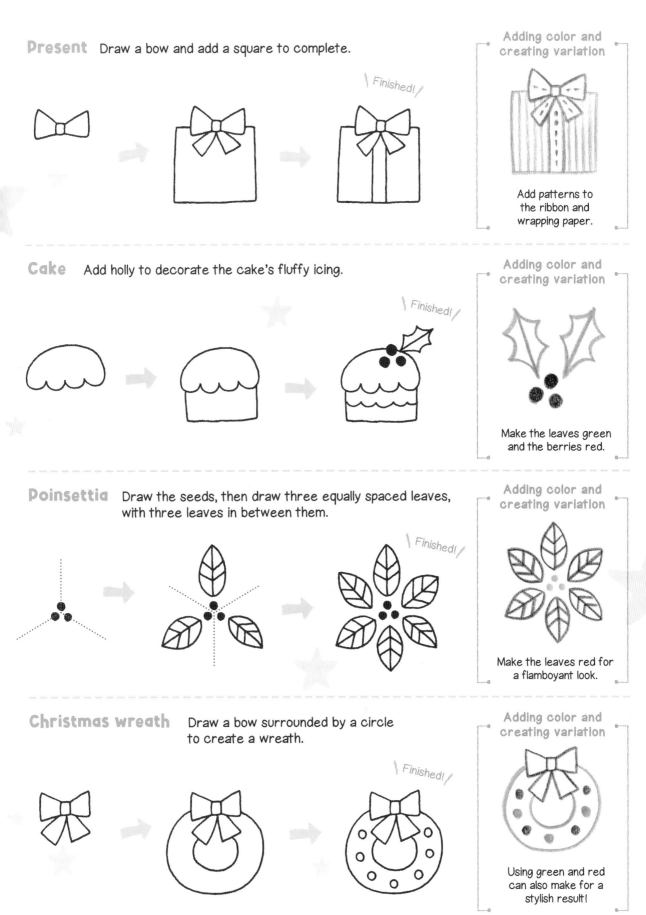

\ Finished! /

Add patterns to the ribbon and wrapping paper.

Cake Add holly to decorate the cake's fluffy icing.

\ Finished! /

Make the leaves green and the berries red.

Poinsettia Draw the seeds, then draw three equally spaced leaves, with three leaves in between them.

\ Finished! /

Make the leaves red for a flamboyant look.

Christmas wreath Draw a bow surrounded by a circle to create a wreath.

\ Finished! /

Using green and red can also make for a stylish result!

89

Bucket & cloth

Drape the cloth over the edge of the bucket and draw a drop of water splashing from it.

\ Finished! /

Adding color and creating variation

Add in stitches for a cute result.

Dustpan & broom

Use a semi-circle shape to start drawing both objects.

\ Finished! /

Adding color and creating variation

Try adding dust and the sense of movement.

Lemon

Adding a little bump on each end is key when drawing a lemon.

\ Finished! /

Adding color and creating variation

To show a cross-section, add drops of juice.

Leek

Make the base slightly rounded with the tops cut straight across to form a squared-off look.

\ Finished! /

Adding color and creating variation

Create a slight bulge at the bottom, but not too much of one.

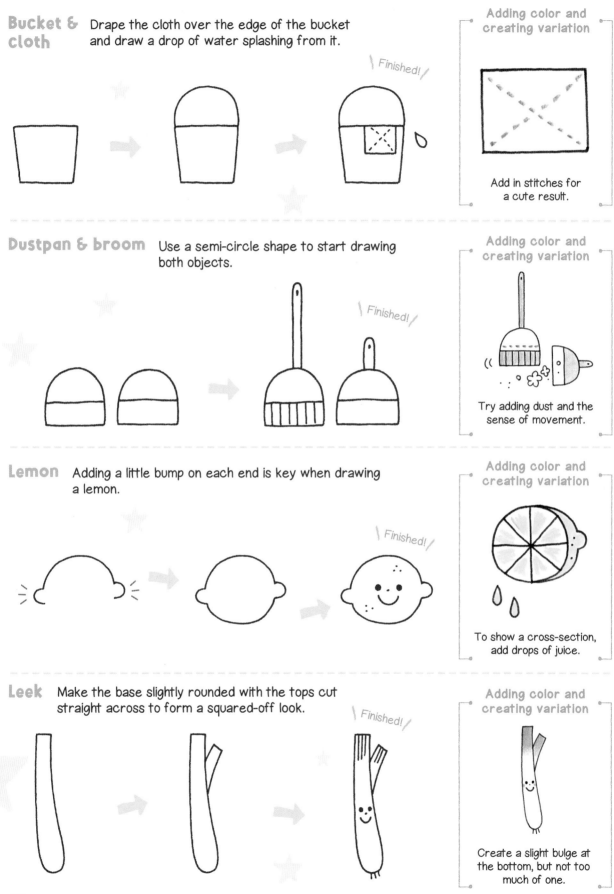

12 DECEMBER

WINTER CARNIVAL

12 HAPPY HOLIDAYS

PEACE ON EARTH

Tis the SEASON

Merry Christmas

★ season's ★ GREETINGS

HOLIDAY Cleanup

Fun Handmade Toys

Kids love handmade toys. Make them even more fun with cute illustrations!

Magnets

Paper clips stick to the magnet on the fishing line. Round off the corners to finish the effect.

Use paint to cover large areas. Mark outlines clearly with a felt-tip pen.

Milk carton puzzles

Materials and tools:
Milk cartons x 4
Illustrations x 6
Clear tape
Scissors

Instructions:
1. Cut illustrations into four equal sections.
2. Make the milk cartons square.
3. Stick illustrations to the milk cartons.

(Expert Tip)

Strengthen the milk cartons by putting the leftover sections inside when making the puzzles.

Fishing   hamburger = p.106, dog = p.31, airplane = p.122, fish = p.37, shortcake = p.102, candy = p.104
Milk carton puzzle   cat = p.30, sailboat = p.123, tortoise = p.37, bread = p.107, trumpet = p.113, apple = p.86

PART THREE

Let's Draw Everyday Illustrations

These adorable illustrations are of items relating to our daily lives or objects, instruments, articles of clothing, occupations, characters and of course sweet treats. What have we left out? What are other icons of the rhythms and routines of daily life?

Activities

Of the many things we do each day, choose some of the highlights, whatever grabs your imagination or will make a strong drawing.

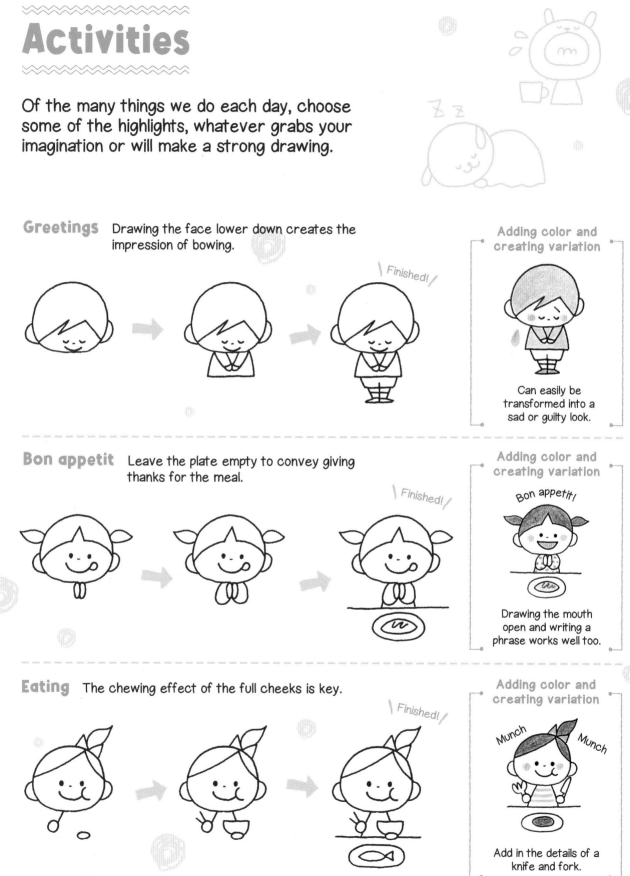

Greetings Drawing the face lower down creates the impression of bowing.

\ Finished! /

Adding color and creating variation

Can easily be transformed into a sad or guilty look.

Bon appetit Leave the plate empty to convey giving thanks for the meal.

\ Finished! /

Adding color and creating variation

Bon appetit!

Drawing the mouth open and writing a phrase works well too.

Eating The chewing effect of the full cheeks is key.

\ Finished! /

Adding color and creating variation

Munch   Munch

Add in the details of a knife and fork.

Gargling

Draw the face high on the head with the mouth wide

\ Finished! /

You could draw the faucet too.

Washing

Draw soap bubbles floating in the air.

\ Finished! /

Add soap or a pump-style bottle.

Nap

Add ZZZs to the sleeping face.

Z z

\ Finished! /

The moon and stars add to the nighttime scene.

Stroller

Make the children's faces peek out from the wagon.

\ Finished! /

Add clouds to indicate the outdoor setting.

95

Occupations

Drawing the specific uniforms and equipment for different jobs makes it easy to distinguish between them.

Police officer
Draw the figure standing at attention with a baton at the waist.

Finished!

Adding color and creating variation
Drawing a dog as a police officer works too.

Doctor
Draw a white coat and place the stethoscope earpieces in the ears.

Finished!

Adding color and creating variation
Draw doctor-related items such as a syringe.

Nurse
Draw a collared dress and the hair tied back.

Finished!

Adding color and creating variation
A nurse's cap works too.

Firefighter The helmet protecting the face is key.

\ Finished! /

Adding color and creating variation

Draw a fire extinguisher too.

Conductor Draw a large face sticking out of the train window.

\ Finished! /

Adding color and creating variation

Draw a bus to go with the driver inside.
*Bus →p.49

Performer The trick is to draw an open mouth with the microphone in the right hand.

\ Finished! /

Adding color and creating variation

Draw musical notes to indicate singing.

Chef Draw the figure holding a frying pan or other cooking utensils and wearing a chef's hat.

\ Finished! /

Adding color and creating variation

The uniform is white. Use accents of color.

Waitress
Add an apron and have her hold a tray.

Finished!

Use a bowtie for a waiter.

Astronaut
Make the face very round. The key is to make the body bulky in its space suit.

Finished!

Scatter stars around to create the sense of outer space.

Soccer player
Draw one foot on the ball and make the figure wink.

Finished!

Draw pentagons to create a soccer ball.

Baseball player
The figure wears a helmet with ear guards and holds a bat.

Finished!

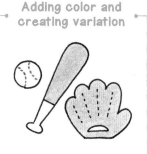

Draw baseball gear such as a ball, bat and glove.

Baker Unlike the chef, the baker wears a softly rounded hat.

\ Finished! /

A bowl and whisk conjure the setting.

Scientist Draw curly hair and glasses.

\ Finished! /

Draw flasks to include an experiment.

Florist Draw a scarf wrapped around her head and flowers in her hand.

\ Finished! /

Drawing flowers in the storefront makes things inviting.

Fishmonger Draw the figure in a headband, long apron and rubber boots, with a fish in one hand.

\ Finished! /

A colorful awning and fish look just right.

99

Stories

These are characters and icons found in stories and fairy tales. Just a few suggestions to get you going. Come up with a few of your own.

Castle Draw large gates, a few triangular sections of roof and a flag.

\ Finished! /

Adding color and creating variation

Add markings on the roof to indicate bricks.

Princess Draw her in a long dress with a tiara.

\ Finished! /

Adding color and creating variation

Make the dress pink.

Prince Make the crown large. He wears voluminous pants and a cape.

\ Finished! /

Adding color and creating variation

Use blue for the pants and decorate the cape.

Pirate The bandanna tied around the head and scar on the face are key.

\ Finished! /

Add a skull to the pirate ship's sail.

Ninja Hide the face as much as possible and create the look of quick movements.

\ Finished! /

Draw ninja stars flying all around.

Red Riding Hood Draw pigtails peeking from the hood and a basket held in both hands.

\ Finished! /

Draw flowers all around to create a fairy-tale atmosphere.

Wolf Draw pointed ears, fangs and a large tail.

\ Finished! /

A drop of saliva adds a scary touch.

Food

Using circles, triangles and squares as foundations, color the food in warm shades to make it look appetizing.

〘 Treats 〙

Birthday cake Add strawberries and candles to the cake.

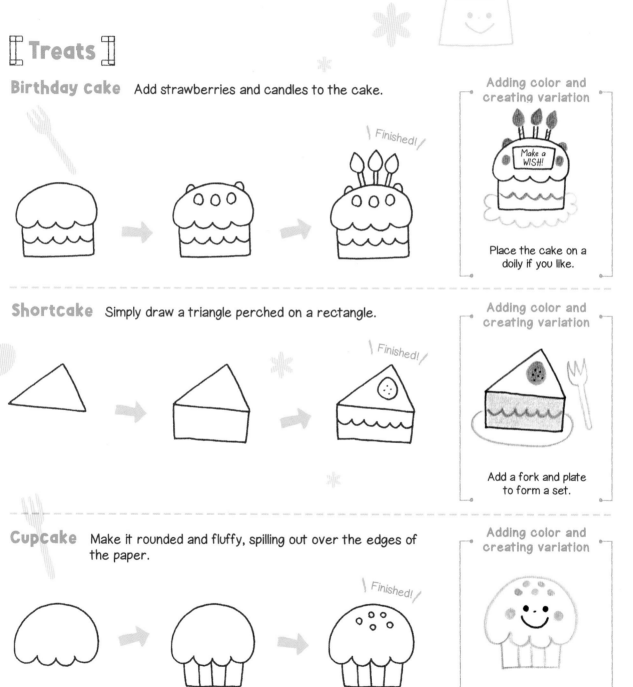

Finished!

Adding color and creating variation

Make a WISH!

Place the cake on a doily if you like.

Shortcake Simply draw a triangle perched on a rectangle.

Finished!

Adding color and creating variation

Add a fork and plate to form a set.

Cupcake Make it rounded and fluffy, spilling out over the edges of the paper.

Finished!

Adding color and creating variation

Add colorful decorations!

Milk Make the bottle rounded and write MILK on it.

\ Finished! /

Adding color and creating variation

Draw arms in for an energetic pose!

Pudding Put a cherry on top to finish it off.

\ Finished! /

Adding color and creating variation

Add a spoon to show it's about to be eaten!

Pancakes Stacking two or three works well. Draw the butter and syrup too.

\ Finished! /

Adding color and creating variation

Use a dark color for the syrup.

Soft serve Make the ice cream slightly pointed at the tip.

\ Finished! /

Adding color and creating variation

Round off the ice cream for a regular cone.

103

All sorts of
yummy things

We love treats!

Two scoops

Tweak the
shortcake

Cheesecake

Candy

Chocolate cake

Pie

Fish-shaped cake

Cream puff

Lollipop

Cookies

Cake balls

Add droplets to
show fizz!

Chocolate

Make the hole
into a mouth!

Soft drink

Lemonade

Popsicle

Rice cracker

Donut

⟦ Meals ⟧

Rice Draw rice so that it's fluffy and piled high.

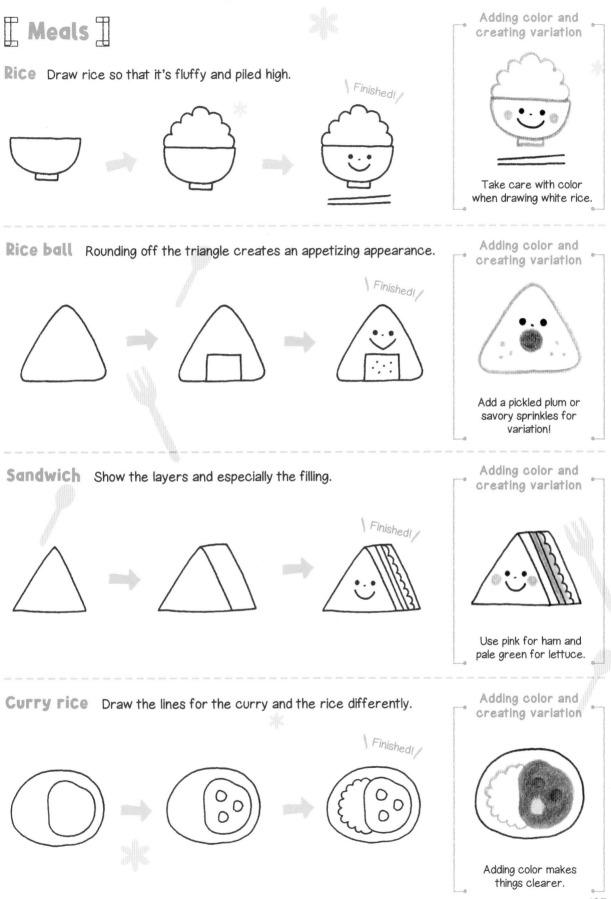

\ Finished! /

Adding color and creating variation

Take care with color when drawing white rice.

Rice ball Rounding off the triangle creates an appetizing appearance.

\ Finished! /

Adding color and creating variation

Add a pickled plum or savory sprinkles for variation!

Sandwich Show the layers and especially the filling.

\ Finished! /

Adding color and creating variation

Use pink for ham and pale green for lettuce.

Curry rice Draw the lines for the curry and the rice differently.

\ Finished! /

Adding color and creating variation

Adding color makes things clearer.

105

Fried egg
Make the yolk round and loosely shape the egg white.

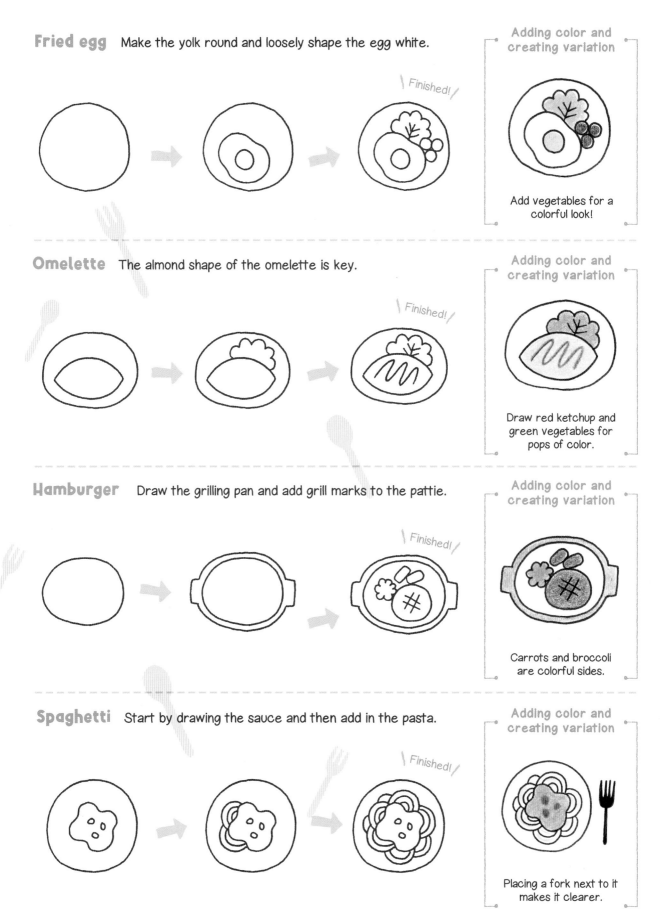

\ Finished! /

Adding color and creating variation

Add vegetables for a colorful look!

Omelette
The almond shape of the omelette is key.

\ Finished! /

Adding color and creating variation

Draw red ketchup and green vegetables for pops of color.

Hamburger
Draw the grilling pan and add grill marks to the pattie.

\ Finished! /

Adding color and creating variation

Carrots and broccoli are colorful sides.

Spaghetti
Start by drawing the sauce and then add in the pasta.

\ Finished! /

Adding color and creating variation

Placing a fork next to it makes it clearer.

All sorts of yummy things

Fun mealtimes

Roll

White bread

Chocolate horn

Hot dog split octopus-style

Shish kebab

Sushi

Salmon roe

Omelette sushi

Ramen

Tuna

Cucumber roll

Fried shrimp

Green tea

Change what the food is saying depending on where it's from

French fries

Vegan meatballs

Hello

Hamburger

G'day!

Chicken nugget

Rice bowl

Pizza

Playtime

Round the edges of instruments and toys so they look appealingly hands-on.

〔 Toys 〕

Bricks
Stack triangles and squares or scatter shapes around.

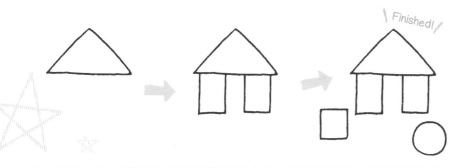

\ Finished! /

Adding color and creating variation

Use various colors for contrasting effect.

Doll
Make the arms and legs simple for a realistic shape.

\ Finished! /

Adding color and creating variation

Alter the hairstyle, bow and clothes for different dolls!

Robot
Use squares and rectangles for all the components.

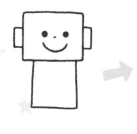

\ Finished! /

Adding color and creating variation

Choose industrial sci-fi colors.

Watering can   Add dots to the round spout section for a realistic look.

\ Finished! /

Adding color and creating variation

Draw droplets falling off the end.

Trowel   Round off the triangle section to soften the edges.

\ Finished! /

Adding color and creating variation

Add a rake to form a set, with the handles in different colors.

Ball   Draw the lines inside the ball curving inward, for a rounded look.

\ Finished! /

Adding color and creating variation

Use a separate color for each band.

Origami   Drawing the individual pieces of paper and the fold lines is key.

\ Finished! /

\ Finished! /

Adding color and creating variation

Make the fronts and backs of the papers different colors.

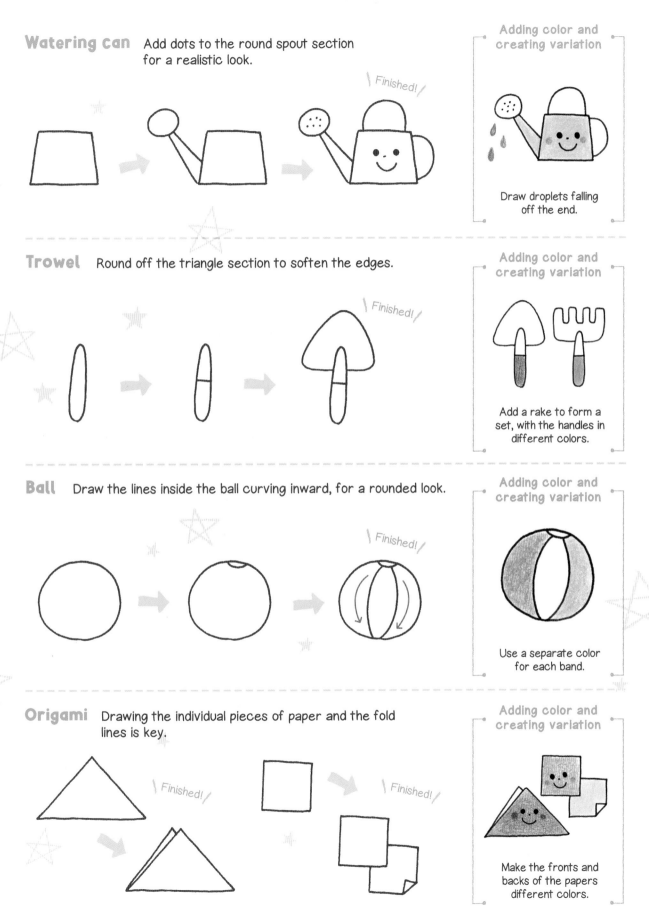

Glue Draw a solid, cylindrical shape.

Finished!

Adding color and creating variation

Create a tube of your own design and coloration.

Scissors Round the ends to make them safe.

Finished!

Adding color and creating variation

Open the blades to make it look like they're cutting.

Crayon Include the paper wrapper wound around the crayon.

Finished!

Adding color and creating variation

Add expressions for a playful look!

Paint The curved section and hole for the fingers to hold the palette is key.

Finished!

Adding color and creating variation

Add several colors for a realistic look.

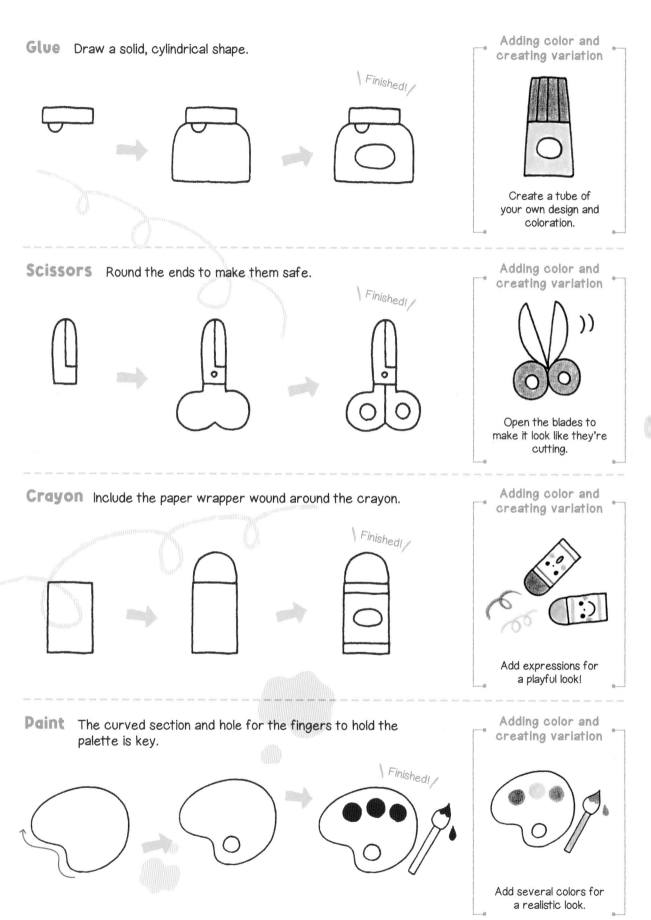

〖 Play equipment 〗

Sand castle Draw dots on two stacked semi-circles with a trowel poking out.

\ Finished! /

Adding color and creating variation

Draw a circle around the picture to create a sandbox.

Slide Draw the slide and ladder diagonally on each side of the structure.

\ Finished! /

Adding color and creating variation

Draw trees in the background to create a playground.

Swings Start with the supports, add the crossbar, then the two swings.

\ Finished! /

Adding color and creating variation

Draw clouds to convey the outdoors.

Medals podium Draw a quadrangle with rounded corners.

\ Finished! /

Adding color and creating variation

Include multi-colored, numbered tiers.

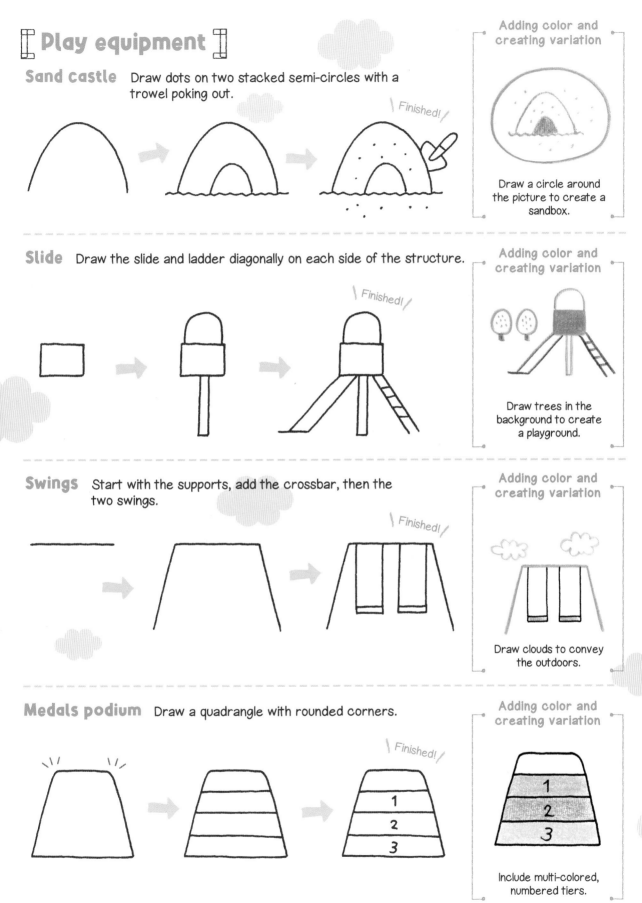

〖 Instrument 〗

Castanets   Stack two circles and add a string tied in a bow.

\ Finished! /

Adding color and creating variation

Color them red and blue to set them apart.

Maracas   Draw a large circle and add stripes.

\ Finished! /

Adding color and creating variation

(( ))

Draw two shaking as if there were one in each hand.

Tambourine   Make the body section flat and add semi-circular cymbals around the edges.

\ Finished! /

Adding color and creating variation

★ ★

Adding stars indicates it's being played.

Bells   Draw only a few bells and make them on the large side.

\ Finished! /

Adding color and creating variation

))

Add movement lines to suggest ringing bells.

Triangle Draw a triangle with one part left open.

\ Finished! /

Adding color and creating variation

Use gray for the metal.

Trumpet Use a large triangle for the bell section.

\ Finished! /

Adding color and creating variation

Add musical notes and make it colorful.

Xylophone The bars run from longest on the left to shortest on the right.

\ Finished! /

Adding color and creating variation

Add the mallets with the heads facing in.

Whistle The protruding section is oblong while the main body is round. Draw the hole too.

\ Finished! /

Adding color and creating variation

Add zigzag lines to convey a loud sound.

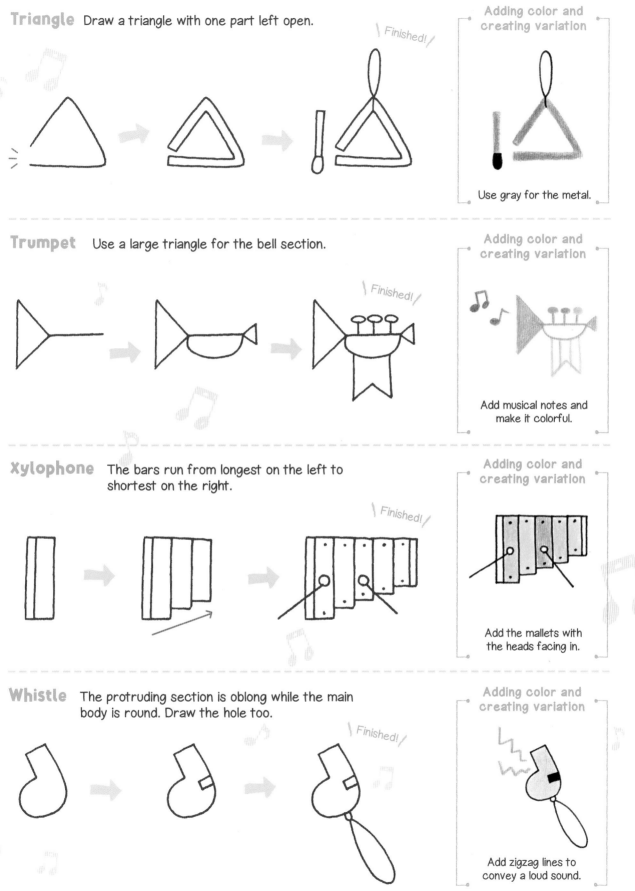

Items Used at School

Add bows and stars to clothing and draw faces on crockery for a cute look.

〚 Clothes 〛

Bag Rounding off the corners of the oblong gives it a compact shape.

\ Finished! /

Adding color and creating variation

Yellow and navy make for a strong color scheme.

Hat Include a rounded crown and a short brim.

\ Finished! /

Adding color and creating variation

Use dark colors for fall/winter and light colors for spring/summer.

Underwear Take out rounded sections to form the neckline and armholes.

\ Finished! /

\ Finished! /

Adding color and creating variation

Draw a star for the boys' version.

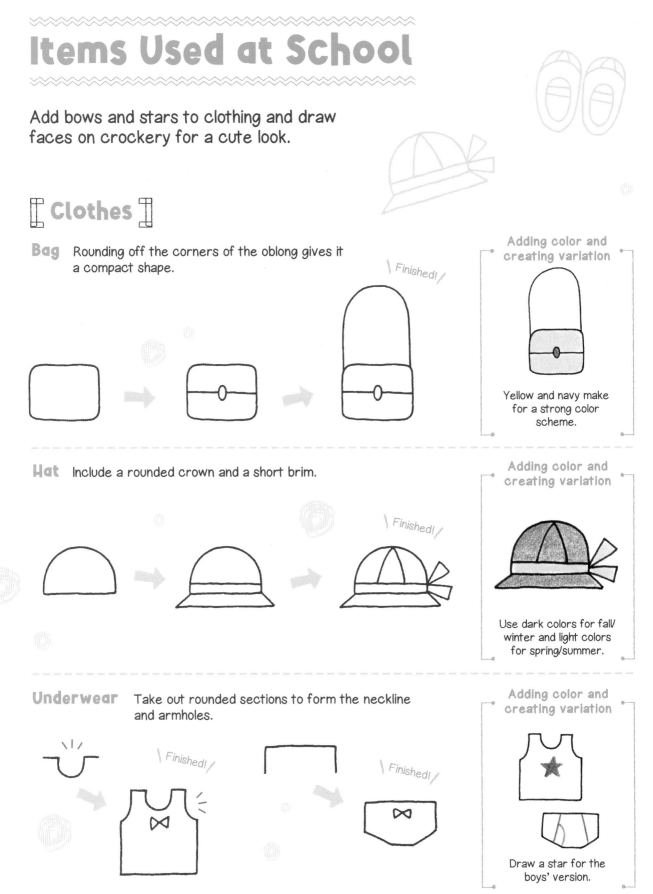

114

Socks Give the toes and heels circular, curvy edges.

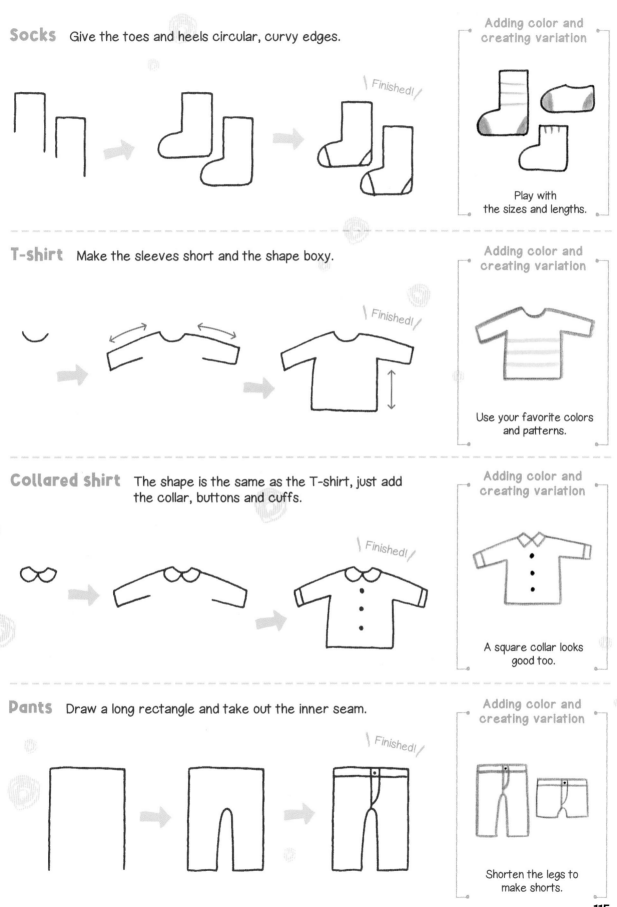

\ Finished! /

Adding color and creating variation

Play with the sizes and lengths.

T-shirt Make the sleeves short and the shape boxy.

\ Finished! /

Adding color and creating variation

Use your favorite colors and patterns.

Collared shirt The shape is the same as the T-shirt, just add the collar, buttons and cuffs.

\ Finished! /

Adding color and creating variation

A square collar looks good too.

Pants Draw a long rectangle and take out the inner seam.

\ Finished! /

Adding color and creating variation

Shorten the legs to make shorts.

Slippers Round off the front, adding in the oval foothole.

\ Finished! /

Adding color and creating variation

Try using different colors for the tips.

Shoes Draw the opening of the shoe and make the sole flat.

\ Finished! /

Adding color and creating variation

Tweak things slightly to create different styles.

Swimsuit (girl's) Make the hem short and floaty.

\ Finished! /

Adding color and creating variation

Add a bow and patterns for a realistic look.

Swimsuit (boy's) Add a drawstring to the shorts.

\ Finished! /

\ Finished! /

Adding color and creating variation

A swim cap and simple stripes complete it.

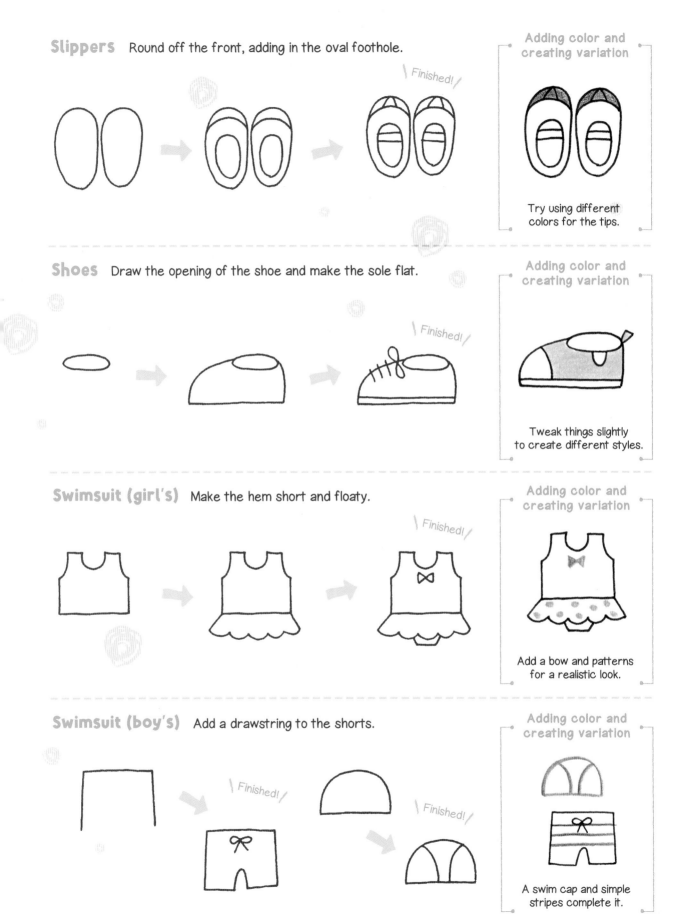

⟦ Handheld items ⟧

Spoon   Give the spoon a large rounded head for an adorable result.

\ Finished! /

Adding color and creating variation

Use zigzag lines on the top to make a spork.

Fork   Make two indentations along the top to create a fork.

\ Finished! /

Adding color and creating variation

Add a knife to make a set.

Chopsticks   Make the tips narrow and the tops slightly thick.

\ Finished! /

Adding color and creating variation

Put them in a box that can go with a bento.

Washcloth   Make the loop wide and the cloth diamond-shaped.

\ Finished! /

Adding color and creating variation

A simple design yields a charming result.

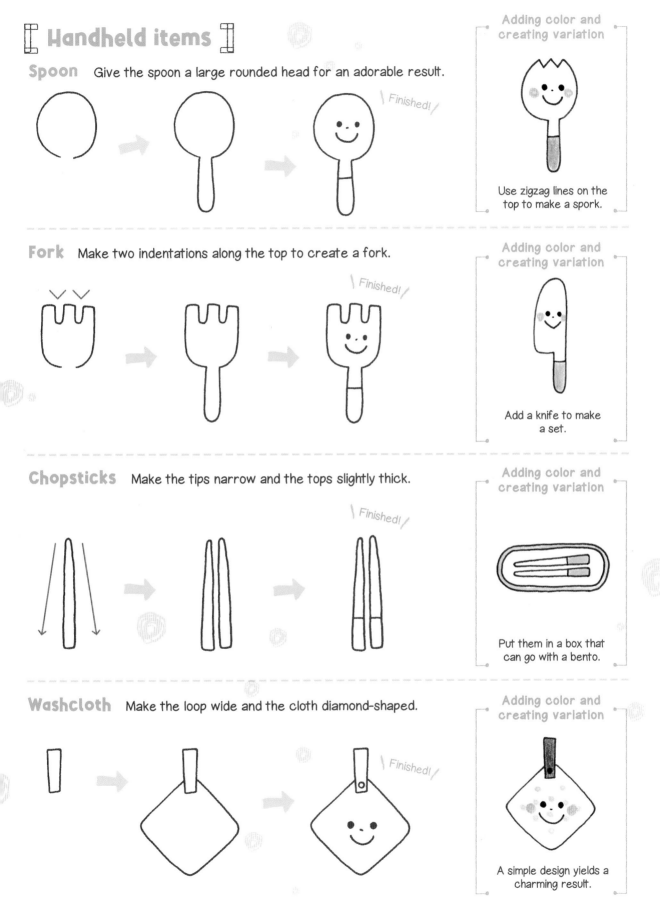

Toothbrush

Round off the ends of the handle and use zigzags for the bristles.

\ Finished! /

Adding color and creating variation

Draw toothpaste to make a set.

Cup

Exaggerate the mug's size and include the beverage inside.

\ Finished! /

Adding color and creating variation

Fill it with water or a soft drink.

Feeding bottle

Make the base flat with the three rounded segments layered above.

\ Finished! /

Adding color and creating variation

Change the color of the measuring lines for fun.

Shopping bag

Draw a large rectangle then add thick straps.

\ Finished! /

Adding color and creating variation

JODI

Add a name tag for a personalized bag.

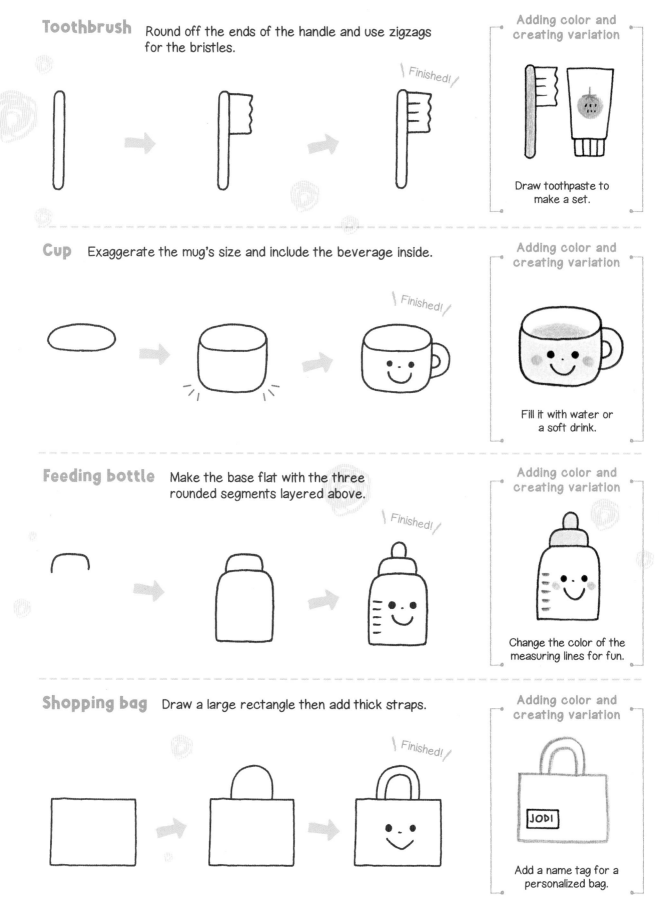

⟦ Other items ⟧

Potty Add two handles to the bird's head.

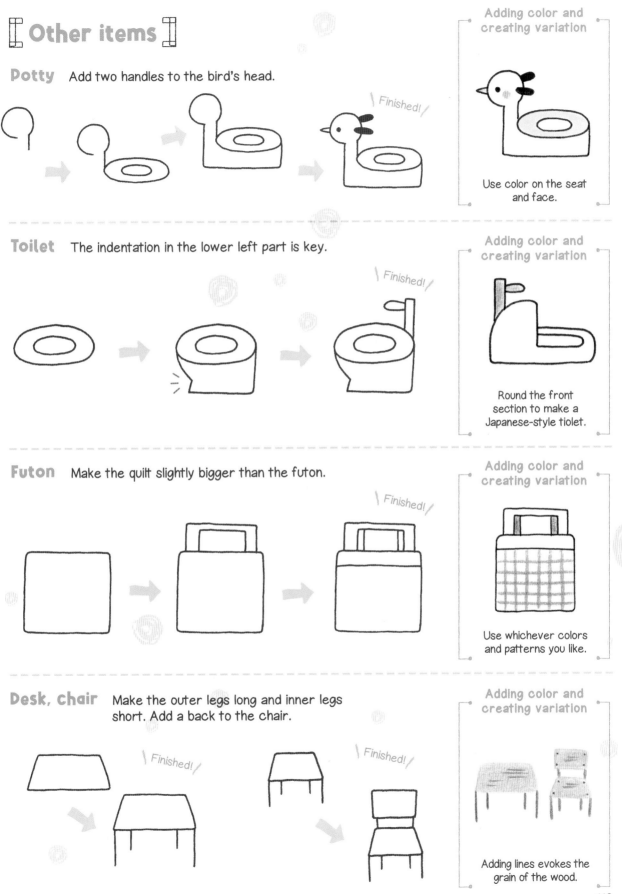

\ Finished! /

Use color on the seat and face.

Toilet The indentation in the lower left part is key.

\ Finished! /

Adding color and creating variation

Round the front section to make a Japanese-style toilet.

Futon Make the quilt slightly bigger than the futon.

\ Finished! /

Adding color and creating variation

Use whichever colors and patterns you like.

Desk, chair Make the outer legs long and inner legs short. Add a back to the chair.

\ Finished! /

\ Finished! /

Adding color and creating variation

Adding lines evokes the grain of the wood.

Vehicles

Start with basic shapes then build from there, adding a sense of dynamism and flow to your drawings of vehicles and things on the go.

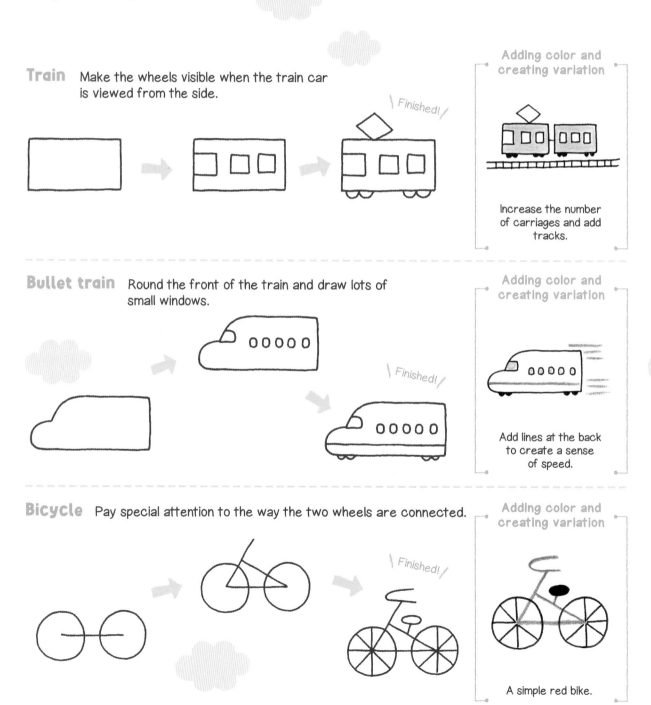

Train Make the wheels visible when the train car is viewed from the side.

\ Finished! /

Adding color and creating variation

Increase the number of carriages and add tracks.

Bullet train Round the front of the train and draw lots of small windows.

o o o o o

\ Finished! /

o o o o o

Adding color and creating variation

o o o o o

Add lines at the back to create a sense of speed.

Bicycle Pay special attention to the way the two wheels are connected.

\ Finished! /

Adding color and creating variation

A simple red bike.

Truck Create a large cargo space in back.

\ Finished! /

Adding color and creating variation

Color in the body and use only stripes for the cargo section.

Ambulance Start with a rectangle, angling off the upper-left quadrant.

\ Finished! /

Adding color and creating variation

Make the body white and the lights red.

Fire engine Draw a long ladder and a coiled hose.

\ Finished! /

Adding color and creating variation

Use red for the body and zigzags for the siren.

Tricycle The key is to draw the tricycle so all three wheels are visible.

\ Finished! /

Adding color and creating variation

A highlight color stands out against the black.

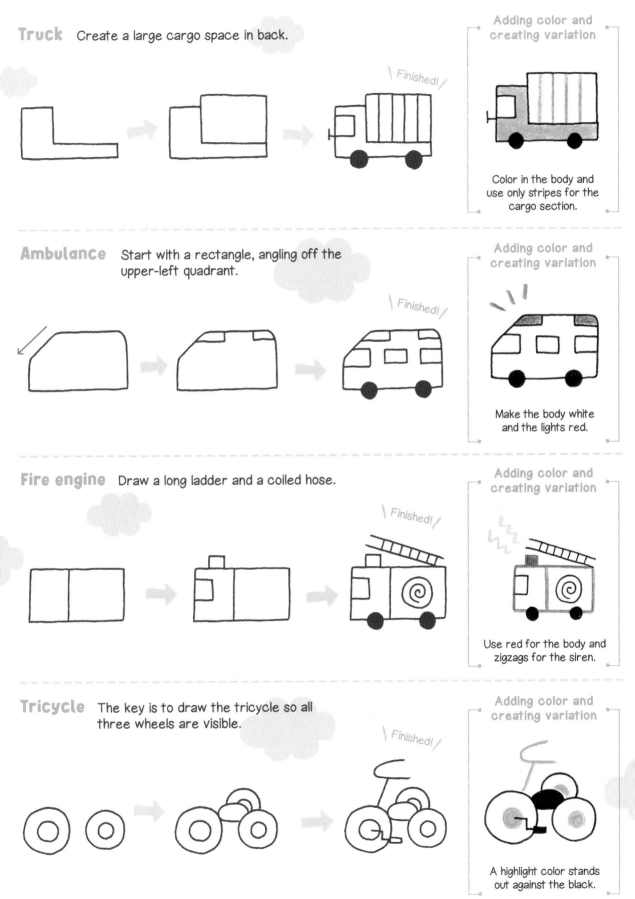

121

Unicycle Draw a large wheel and small pedals.

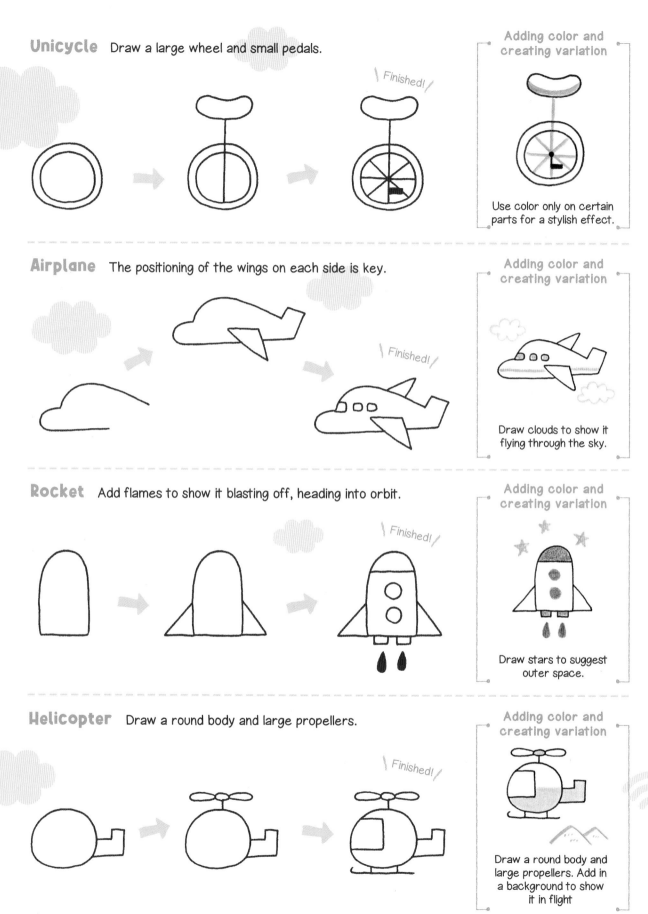

\ Finished! /

Adding color and creating variation

Use color only on certain parts for a stylish effect.

Airplane The positioning of the wings on each side is key.

\ Finished! /

Adding color and creating variation

Draw clouds to show it flying through the sky.

Rocket Add flames to show it blasting off, heading into orbit.

\ Finished! /

Adding color and creating variation

Draw stars to suggest outer space.

Helicopter Draw a round body and large propellers.

\ Finished! /

Adding color and creating variation

Draw a round body and large propellers. Add in a background to show it in flight

Hot air ballooon
Draw a large circle and use lines to connect it to the basket.

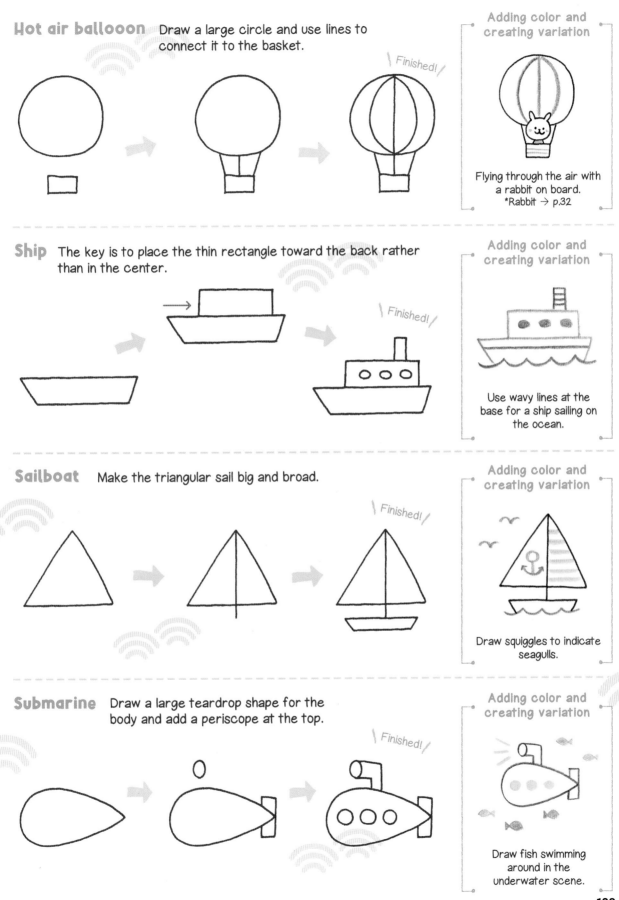

\ Finished! /

Adding color and creating variation

Flying through the air with a rabbit on board.
*Rabbit → p.32

Ship
The key is to place the thin rectangle toward the back rather than in the center.

\ Finished! /

Adding color and creating variation

Use wavy lines at the base for a ship sailing on the ocean.

Sailboat
Make the triangular sail big and broad.

\ Finished! /

Adding color and creating variation

Draw squiggles to indicate seagulls.

Submarine
Draw a large teardrop shape for the body and add a periscope at the top.

\ Finished! /

Adding color and creating variation

Draw fish swimming around in the underwater scene.

Peekaboo & What Am I?

Let's try making two kinds of stick puppets with front and reverse sides.

Stick puppets

Peekaboo!

What am I? Can you guess?

Stick puppets   cat = p.30, rabbit = p.32, elephant = p.34, grapes = p.77, bee = p.59, tulip = p.57

Ideas for Combining Illustrations

\ All sorts of uses /

\ Introducing /

Notices & announcements

Here are headlines you can use for announcements in newsletters, posters and flyers.

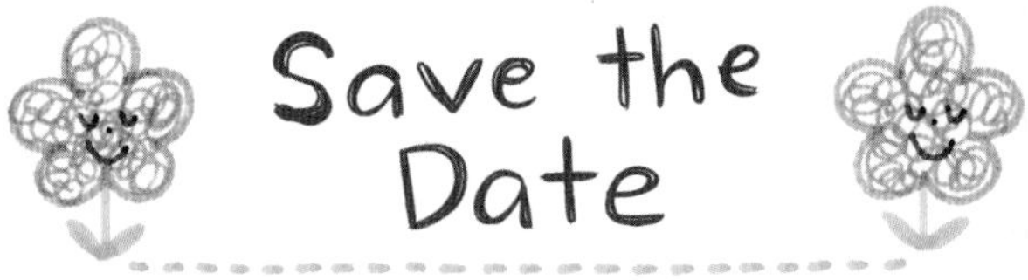

DON'T FORGET

NEWS

TODAY

Save the Date

VOTE

Spring Break

DRIVE SAFELY

WELCOME!

SCHOOL RECITAL

Celebrations, birthdays, rewards

Use a combination of illustrations and words
for birthdays, certificates and so on.

PEACE

Graduation Day

Shh! It's a Surprise PARTY!

Shh! It's a SURPRISE PARTY

0 1 2 3 4 5 6

GOOD LUCK!

KING for a day

It's a PARTY!

SUMMER Vacation

PET Adoption

Various illustrations

Copy these drawings to use for various illustrations.

- Measuring weight
- Measuring height
- Occupied
- Early riser
- Early to bed
- "Wait your turn" or "Line up!"
- Cleaning up
- Watch out for kids playing
- Don't get a stomach ache
- Look both ways before crossing

*Only the outline is provided for ease of copying, alterations and coloring in.

"Books to Span the East and West"

Tuttle Publishing was founded in 1832 in the small New England town of Rutland, Vermont [USA]. Our core values remain as strong today as they were then—to publish best-in-class books which bring people together one page at a time. In 1948, we established a publishing office in Japan—and Tuttle is now a leader in publishing English-language books about the arts, languages and cultures of Asia. The world has become a much smaller place today and Asia's economic and cultural influence has grown. Yet the need for meaningful dialogue and information about this diverse region has never been greater. Over the past seven decades, Tuttle has published thousands of books on subjects ranging from martial arts and paper crafts to language learning and literature—and our talented authors, illustrators, designers and photographers have won many prestigious awards. We welcome you to explore the wealth of information available on Asia at **www.tuttlepublishing.com**.

Published by Tuttle Publishing, an imprint of Periplus Editions (HK) Ltd.

www.tuttlepublishing.com

KANTAN! KAWAII! KAMO SAN NO HOIKU NO ILLUST 12-KAGETSU
Copyright © 2017 Kamo
English translation rights arranged with SHINSEI Publishing Co., Ltd through Japan UNI Agency, Inc., Tokyo

Library of Congress Cataloging-in-Publication Data in process
ISBN 978-4-8053-1696-2

English Translation © 2022 Periplus Editions (HK) Ltd.

The original Japanese edition contains handwritten characters within the illustrations. In the English edition, these handwritten Japanese characters have been replaced, where necessary, with standard fonts and typefaces.

25 24 23 22   10 9 8 7 6 5 4 3 2 1

Printed in China   2204EP

Distributed by

North America, Latin America & Europe
Tuttle Publishing
364 Innovation Drive
North Clarendon, VT 05759-9436 U.S.A.
Tel: 1 (802) 773-8930
Fax: 1 (802) 773-6993
info@tuttlepublishing.com
www.tuttlepublishing.com

Japan
Tuttle Publishing
Yaekari Building 3rd Floor
5-4-12 Osaki
Shinagawa-ku
Tokyo 141-0032
Tel: (81) 3 5437-0171
Fax: (81) 3 5437-0755
sales@tuttle.co.jp
www.tuttle.co.jp

Asia Pacific
Berkeley Books Pte. Ltd.
3 Kallang Sector, #04-01
Singapore 349278
Tel: (65) 6741 2178
Fax: (65) 6741 2179
inquiries@periplus.com.sg
www.tuttlepublishing.com